COPING WITH
anxiety

COPING WITH
anxiety

John D. Jess

Baker Book House
Grand Rapids, Michigan

FOREWORD

We need the capacity and compassion to relate to others, to put ourselves in their places, to view things through their eyes. How can we hope to reach them for Christ unless we do?

These words from John D. Jess, founder and Director of *The Chapel of the Air* broadcast, help to explain the phenomenal growth of the program in recent years. That Jess communicates on a very special wavelength with people of every age, culture, and social strata is evidenced by his "feedback" mail from listeners. People from every walk of life respond to his direct, one-to-one approach as he ministers across America and overseas each weekday.

The following radio messages have been transcribed exactly as delivered on the broadcast. The style is conversational rather than literary; the material has been garnered from many sources. May your heart be warmed, encouraged, and *stretched* as you read.

The Editors

CONTENTS

Have we taken God's burdens
upon ourselves
because He is not big enough?

1 COPING WITH ANXIETY

Anxiety is the official emotion of our age. Practically everything we do is colored by it. "The twentieth century," writes psychologist J. Marmor in *The Encyclopedia of Mental Health*, "is more anxiety-ridden than any other era in history since the Middle Ages."

The reasons for this are legion. We live amid such rapid and far-reaching technological changes, we become anxious just trying to "keep up." Add to this our troubled economy, the many explosive world situations, the threat of overpopulation, the burgeoning crime wave, the increasing ability of scientists to manipulate human behavior, the changing values of youth, etc., and remaining free from anxiety becomes a herculean feat.

Even those who somehow manage to ignore the daily news have no guarantee against anxiety. They may worry about the forthcoming trip to the dentist, or a driver's test, or an undiagnosed illness. So anxiety touches all of us in one way or another, and it always takes its toll.

Psychologists tell us there are two primary kinds of anxiety—specific and free-floating. An example of specific anxiety would be claustrophobia, the fear of tightly enclosed places. There are, in fact, some thirty-eight kinds of phobia, each an exaggerated and persistent dread of, or aversion to, something.

Free-floating anxieties are those that cannot be pinned down. Persons suffering from such anxieties don't know why they feel as they do. They just live in constant dread of something happening to them. We have all read or heard of rich people, fearing poverty, suffering from malnutrition, dressing in rags, living in dingy quarters, and dying with a million dollars or more stuffed in mattresses or buried in tin cans. Such people are always highly troubled, always neurotic, often recluses.

Sigmund Freud was the first person to make a distinction between normal and neurotic anxiety. We are all aware that there is normal anxiety. It occurs when there is real danger, or cause for concern. When the Apollo 12 moonshot got in trouble, the astronauts, knowing there was a possibility they would be lost in space, were understandably and justifiably anxious. The danger they faced was very real. But a neurotic kind of anxiety sees problems and dangers when they exist only in the mind.

But real or imagined, anxiety always produces adverse physical reactions. The heart speeds up; there may be an abnormal tightness in the throat, a shortness of breath, and frequently loss of sleep and appetite. And, for your information, fear can actually make a person's hair stand on end! It can also drain the blood from the face and cause "goose bumps" to form on the skin.

Why is anxiety so common? Why has it become "the official emotion of our age?" Dr. Ernest R. Hilgard, past president of the American Psychological Association, suggests the following reasons:

The causes of contemporary anxiety are complex: Two world wars within our century, and a cold war persisting since the last one; enormous mobilities of peoples, geographically and economically, disturbing the sense of rootedness; shifting values so that we are uncertain about child-rearing practices, about moral standards, about religious beliefs.

This of course fails to explain why some children are afraid to go to school or stay with a babysitter, why many adults are afraid in the presence of snakes, or why many good Christians are afraid to share their faith with others.

Actually, anxiety has two or three primary causes. First, many people learn to be afraid. For example, the mother who is terrified by storms will almost certainly pass that fear along to her children. Often people who have been victims of a serious automobile accident will forever thereafter be on "needles and pins" in a car. Many war pilots never take the controls of a plane again when they return to civilian life because of the dangers they encountered in combat. So we do learn anxiety through experience; in fact, those who do not learn it seldom live long. Normal anxiety is the product of education, experience, and mature judgment. We warn little children about crossing streets, playing with matches, accepting rides from strangers, etc. We warn them because as yet they have not learned the dangers inherent in these situations.

Their parents, on the other hand, can get all tensed up and unnerved watching a telecast which shows crowds engaged in anarchy, or a terrible catastrophe, while the child plays happily and unconcernedly on the floor. He doesn't comprehend the horror of the situation.

I suppose we could all live in a state of perpetual panic if God had not made it possible for us to shut off (or out) a lot of potential dangers. Although we are constantly surrounded by anxiety-arousing issues, we cannot afford to ponder them consciously. If we did, we would be, as the kids say, constantly "uptight" and "strung out."

The disturbing thing is that many who have the least reason to worry, do. Jesus, addressing His disciples, said, "Therefore do not be anxious about your life . . ." (Matt. 6:25). He consistently condemned worry and anxiety. So did Paul. In Philippians 4:6,7, the apostle wrote:

> Have no anxiety about anything, but in everything by prayer and supplication with thanksgiving let your requests be made known to God. And the peace of God, which passes all understanding, will keep your hearts and your minds in Christ Jesus.

It is time we Christians learned that anxiety (in the form of fret and worry) is nothing short of sin. It is an announcement to the world that we lack faith in the sovereignty of God. When we are anxious over conditions, or the state of the world, we are saying they have passed beyond God's control. We are saying we have taken life's burdens on ourselves because God is not big enough for them. This, in effect, makes us our own god; so we can thereafter expect anxiety to increase. Godlessness and anxiety are colleagues. Where you find one you are almost certain to find the other.

Concern, on the other hand, is something else. While Christians are not to be anxious (worried), they should be concerned. Jesus never worried, but He was concerned. Once He looked down upon Jerusalem and wept, for He knew its million souls, because of their spiritual indifference, would suffer vanquishment. Paul never worried about the beatings he had to endure, or the cold and hunger he underwent, or the persecution he bore. But he was deeply concerned about the churches he had established and the welfare of the members. This is evidenced by the terminology of his letters.

"The end intention of the gospel," writes a Christian psychologist (W. E. Oates) "is to release man from the egocentricities and anxieties of life and . . . to a concern for the welfare of others."

Both psychology and the Bible agree that there is nothing wrong with being concerned about the problems of life; indeed, it is a healthy sign if anxiety is focused on the needs and welfare of others. But there are two extremes. Some become so inured to life's problems that they become immobilized and useless. On the other hand, some become so excessively concerned that they suffer physically, mentally, and spiritually.

I receive literally hundreds of letters, papers, documents, periodicals, brochures, tracts, books, magazines, etc., whose intent it is to "awaken" me (and presumably others) to the perils of our day. These well-meaning individuals encourage me to interject myself into political campaigns, to expose culprits in high places, and, ostensibly, to do something on a national scale to deter or stop the evil that is admittedly part and parcel of our socio-political structure.

Now I agree with some (not all) of the conclusions these alarmists have reached. I am aware that this nation is in grave danger from despoiling forces we are either tolerating or encouraging: the smut peddlers, the criminal element, alien political ideologies, cults, etc. But I came to realize long ago that these are burdens I cannot carry. I cannot become responsible for the actions and activities of those bent on tearing this nation apart. I can warn, but there my responsibility stops. If I took the problems of the world to bed with me, I would never have another night's sleep as long as I live!

There is a hymn titled, "This Is My Father's World." This is true, although there is a sense in which it is the devil's world (the Bible refers to him as "the god of this age"). But we Christians must never assume that God has

13

lost control, that He is nonplussed, frustrated, defeated. The moment we yield to that concept our purpose for being is surrendered and our message becomes one of defeat, not victory!

Actually, the love of God is the best and most viable antidote for fear. I like the Phillips translation of I John 4:18:

> Love contains no fear—indeed, fully developed love expels every particle of fear, for fear always contains some of the torture of feeling guilty. This means that the man who lives in fear has not yet had his love perfected.

Because God loves us, we can lay every burdensome fear our environment places on us on Him. Because the believer is secure in Him, nothing can ultimately hurt him. Paul assures us that nothing can separate us from His love, because "we are more than conquerors through Him who loved us" (Rom. 8:37).

Does God love me? I believe He does. Therefore I stand on Philippians 4:6,7:

> Don't worry about anything; instead, pray about everything; tell God your needs and don't forget to thank Him for His answers. If you do this you will experience God's peace, which is far more wonderful than the human mind can understand. His peace will keep your thoughts and your hearts quiet and at rest as you trust in Jesus Christ. *(The Living Bible)*

*Jesus sent His disciples into the world
to rise above it,
to conquer it!*

2 DEFINING A CHRISTIAN

There's no doubt about it . . . ideas vary as to what a "good" Christian is. Some think you have to act a little crazy to be a "good" Christian. Others think you should cry a little when you talk about Jesus, or perhaps pray with ear-splitting fervency. Others associate a "good" Christian with not doing much of anything, just staying out of trouble and piously clucking the tongue over sin.

In our country there are even areas in which much importance is attached to handling venomous snakes and working oneself into a frenzy during "gospel meetings."

Since God didn't make me a judge over men, I'll not assume that responsibility, but I can say without fear of successful contradiction that there is not a trace of such foolishness in the New Testament! Even on the day of Pentecost, when the disciples were introduced to the Person and power of the Holy Spirit, there was no abnormal behavior. To be sure they were accused of having imbibed too freely, but that was merely because their accusers had never encountered people like them before. The newly empowered disciples didn't really emulate drunks. They didn't wobble and weave. They didn't curse and slur their words. They didn't speak incoherently. The only "unusual" thing about their behavior was their boldness and their ability to be understood in a variety of languages. It would take a mind fertile with imagination to connect that sort of behavior with drunkenness!

I have been a Christian for forty years and I can tell you from personal observation and experience that Christianity does not produce "screwballs." Paul, writing to Timothy, said, "God has not given us the spirit of fear; but of power, and of love, and of a sound mind" (II Tim. 1:7). While some of the newer translations substitute the word "discipline" for the term "a sound mind," the Greek term is *sōp*, meaning "soundness of mind," or "prudence." And that is precisely how it is translated in the King James Version, the version that is uncannily correct in most instances!

I once read that "the gospel of Jesus Christ never fathers a fanatic." I know some people say a religious fanatic is merely a "fan" of Jesus, but without getting into the finer points of semantics, I'd like to say that most people consider a fanatic a "kook," so I'm not willing to concede that real Christians are fanatics. I don't say the world will understand them, or be tolerant of them, but I don't believe a Christian needs to make a fool of himself, even for Jesus' sake. Paul, writing to the Corinthians, said, "Let all things be done decently and in order" (I Cor. 14:40). I gather from this that all unseemly behavior has an author other than the Holy Spirit.

I remember, as a young Christian, there were occasions when neighbors living adjacent to churches where there was extreme emotionalism had to sometimes call the police to quell late-night boisterousness. That causes me to burn with shame for the sake of the sane gospel I love! I am not opposed to enthusiasm, but I believe we can be enthusiastic without being obnoxious. There is nothing on earth more sane, more appealing, more con-

16

victing, than Christians under the control of God's Holy Spirit!

It also embarrasses me when the person of Jesus Christ is tied in with preaching that can only give untutored listeners a grotesque concept of Him. Preaching, from sermon content to voice inflection, should be as attractive as the One we represent. Remember, we are the only Christ the world knows. I often ask myself, and I want you to ask yourself, "What concept do they have of Him when they watch me and listen to me?"

I am sure the impression some unbelievers get is that they'll have to become a funny-acting oddball if they become a Christian! This should not be, for Jesus was the sanest person who ever lived. Even today He commands the respect of many of the world's greatest intellects. The apostle Paul, named as one of the seven greatest thinkers of history, wrote to the church at Philippi, "Let this mind be in you, which was also in Christ Jesus" (2:5). That means a balanced, controlled, discriminating mind.

Previously I referred to II Timothy 1:7 in which Paul said, "God has not given us the spirit of fear. . . ." In my studies I have found that fear and faith are incompatible. As a Christian, are you showing the world your faith or your fear; your faith or your lack of it? Christians donate millions of dollars annually to foster ministries that play on their fears, that warn year after year of impending doom. Now I'm not intimating that this land of ours is not in danger. Any nation with a religious heritage such as ours that turns its corporate back on the gospel of Jesus Christ as we have is in dire peril; however, we must bear in mind that the New Testament gospel is not a gospel of despair. I consider it a denial of the faith to live habitually in a state of terror. Have we lost confidence in the Christian's ultimate triumph?

I am not saying fear is always a carnal emotion. To have no fear of disease may be to die prematurely. To have no fear of speed may be to fashion one's own casket out of crumpled steel. To have no fear of a loaded gun may be to die of lead poisoning! In the context of self-preservation fear is permissible at times, but I'm not talking about an occasional flash of fright. I'm talking about a climate of timidity or cowardice. Let's face it, some Christians are downright lily-livered! They see potential death and destruction under every bed, around every corner, in every public utterance. They act as if God had lost control of His world.

Jesus' disciples, in a great state of alarm, once awakened Him in a boat that was being storm-tossed. His words to them were, "Why are ye fearful, O ye of little faith?" How could they be frightened with Jesus in the boat? How can we?

The only plausible interpretation of II Timothy 1:7 is that the "sound mind" is a trusting mind. I know many of you need that, for I receive so many letters from people who are in a state of perpetual shock. Their letters sound as if God had abdicated His throne or had been tossed out of heaven! They fear just about everything: ridicule, loneliness, pain, poverty, and even the prospect of death. What good is faith if it doesn't dispel fear? Anyone who can trust Christ for salvation should be able to trust Him afterward. Oh, Christians, stop dying those thousand little deaths every day! If your God is so helpless, so unmindful, how can you recommend Him to others? Jesus sent His disciples into a world dominated by fear, not to join it, but to rise above it, to conquer it!

Someone has said there are four ways to handle fears: rationalize them, deny them, narcotize them, or avoid all situations that might arouse them. But I can't recommend any of these. To rationalize fear is to admit that you are frightened, and that won't help. To deny fear is to say that it doesn't exist, and that's an out-and-out lie. To narcotize fear is the way of an ostrich and a coward.

And to try to avoid any situation that will produce fear (where there is an absence of faith) is an exercise in futility.

The two factors Paul mentions in this connection are love and power. Love needs no explanation, but what about power? I believe this is power that comes not only from being filled with the Holy Spirit, but also the power that comes with good sense. It's virtually impossible to have a powerful life or ministry without the balancing factor of a sharp mind. I don't mean a highly educated mind, or the brain of a genius, but a spiritual mind, the kind Paul calls in I Corinthians 2:16 "the mind of Christ." The mind of Christ, highly educated or not, is a balanced, logical, discriminating, pure, illuminated mind.

Modern psychology teaches that power comes from an understanding of oneself, which certainly is not altogether untrue, but no one has ever been saved from himself by trusting himself. Hitler wasn't. Stalin wasn't. And going back further, Alexander and Napoleon weren't.

What is another characteristic of a sound mind? Love. At the risk of sounding trite, I'll say that to have a sound mind without love is as impossible as it would be for a person to walk around without his bone structure! Love, in a manner of speaking, is the "bone structure" of a sound mind.

Someone has said, "We will learn to love, or we will perish." But how can the world be taught to love without God? "Make love, not war," is an intriguing little slogan, but the love it refers to is not the love that will save the world, but the love that may destroy it!

Love, and a mind sound enough to administer it, are gifts of God. His enemies can never attain to them. The psalmist tells it like it is: "Thou wilt keep him in perfect peace whose mind is stayed on thee; because he trusteth in thee" (26:3).

How desperately the world needs soundness of mind based on the soundness that springs from the love and power of God through Jesus Christ! Those thus endowed I would say are the "good" Christians.

Rivers sometimes become stagnant
in the swamp of custom.

3 THE CHRISTIAN IN A CHANGING WORLD

In a recent radio message I appealed for a return to some of the old standards now so lamentably forsaken. I realize, of course, that we will never do that; we cannot do it, but I appreciated the nostalgia my listeners indulged me. It will, I know, never be more than that.

I do hope, however, that nothing I ever do or say will be construed to mean that I oppose progress or change. That would not only be futile; it would be senile. Change is as inexorable as the seasons. Resisting change would be as silly as trying to dam Niagara with a toothpick.

Perhaps the oldest controversy in history is the struggle between the old and the new, between the past and the future. In age after age there have been those who have tried to retain the status quo as opposed to those who have tried to improve it. The question is, where do Christians fit in this conflict? Where do we stand, and what should be our attitude in times of radical change? This is much more than an academic question; it is something we must make up our minds about, for, like it or not, we are going to live out our lives in an era of unsettledness. Those who talk about a return to "normalcy" should be prepared for deep disappointment, for we will never again live in "normal" times.

The biographer of King Louis XVI said of him, "He was an amiable and upright man and doubtless would have made a good leader in times of peace." Unfortunately however, his ancestors bequeathed him a revolution. And that is where you and I are today. We inherited a revolution, and we're going to live out our days in a furious clash between the old and the new.

When David Rockefeller was named Businessman of the Year, he said: "In [life] today the past is overwhelmed by the future. . . There has occurred a transformation so swift in pace and so profound in social implications that it has outstripped the perception of most historians."

Yes, these are times of swift and profound changes. But where do Christians fit into the picture? Do we go back, or do we go along?

Let me first say that the aware Christian is not allergic to change. If he were, he wouldn't be a Christian. Every true Christian is a "new" person. "If any man be in Christ," wrote the apostle Paul, "he is a new creature: old things are passed away; behold, all things are become new." That means Christians turn their backs on the old and their faces toward the new. And that spells change; it denotes progress.

But what is "progress?" J. Wallace Hamilton epitomized it in this sentence: "All progress is made by the simple technique of building in the present on some foundations of the past, taking the gains of yesterday and going further with them today." That, I would say, is a fair definition of progress. It's keeping the "good" old and adding on the "good" new.

Unfortunately, some people reject everything new. They may not eschew modern conveniences, the brainchildren of our scientists, but they cling to the status quo when it comes to methods of witnessing and wor-shiping. Some people won't listen to anything but "old-fashioned" sermons, by which I assume they mean fire-breathing, foot-stomping, Bible-thumping, superani-mated pulpit gymnastics. They also mean oversimplifica-tions, those most of us used in an era when people accepted them and were satisfied with them.

Let me make it clear that such people are not stupid; they are just naive. They don't understand the modern mentality (which I am not defending), therefore they are not aware that terminology that was meaningful to past generations is meaningless today. There is no law against witnessing for Christ today like it was done thirty or forty years ago, but whoever does so won't get the ear of the masses. He will only be talking to himself and possibly a few others who haven't as yet traded in their horses and buggies!

I am not saying I am keen about the change, but I would rather resign from the ministry than advertise Jesus Christ to this hip generation with 1925 tactics and sepulchral pulpit tones. If I did, I would more likely be called "funny man" than "preacher."

The August 21, 1970, issue of *Christianity Today* contains an excellent article by Jerry W. Haughton en-titled "Incarnational Evangelism." It's a plea for new and better witnessing methods which conform to the times. Haughton bases his arguments on Paul's accom-modation (not compromise) in I Corinthians 9:20-23. I would point out one statement by Dr. Haughton which I consider exceptionally timely:

> Many non-Christians in Western culture have what we might call a "Christian memory:" they respect the Bible as God's message of salvation because of the Christian training they received as children. With these persons we can use the Bible in our witness for Christ. But a growing majority of non-Christians do not respect the Bible as God's Word

and will not permit the Christian to use it in his witness to them. So he has to use a different approach.

The point is that we are living in a postChristian era. People do not respect the Bible as they once did. This doesn't mean we are to deal with them on a non-Biblical basis, but it does mean we must make allowance for their background and must not impose on them the type of witnessing that turns them off.

Let me cite a case in point. I recently conversed with a young university graduate who majored in history. He knew more about the history of the Bible than I do. A woman member of an evangelical church had been witnessing to him, he told me, and trying to persuade him to attend her church. But when she told him that the apostle Paul used the King James Version, it became obvious to him that she was ignorant and thereafter he tried to avoid her. Fifty years ago her ignorance might not have been an issue, but today a junior high-schooler would choke on that one!

This, I realize, is an extreme example, but it underscores the fact that many sincere Christians just aren't "with it," to borrow a colloquialism. They haven't boned up on the times. They are living in another age.

I am not suggesting, understand, that we sever ties completely with the past. That would be suicidal. Our roots are in it; we dare not ignore it. The student who starts out in the chemical lab with contempt for the past, relying on his own judgment without regard for past experiments, may lose his head—literally! All scientific advancement is made possible by past experiments. The New Testament is rooted in the Old. We can never get away from the past, but neither can we afford to stop there. All revolutions are not carried out by bad men trying to destroy the old. Sometimes good men, clinging tenaciously to the past, dam up the forces which ought to flow into the normal procedures of progress.

What I am saying is that rivers sometimes grow stagnant in the swamp of custom!

Who wants to go back to the world of greedy systems, racial bigotry, unregulated colonialism, and imperialism? There is no more reason to preserve them than there is to preserve a ghetto. Isaiah cried, "Make the crooked places straight!" (45:2). When crooked places are made straight in our time, let's thank God for it and join the builders!

I am not asking for blind belief in "progress," or gullible hospitality to everything labeled new. Many things paraded as new are neither new nor true, and certainly not all revolutions denote progress. In fact, Christians deplore many "new" things. We know that what is labeled the "new sexuality" is only age-old immorality, and what is branded the "new theology" is nothing but old, discredited heresy. What I am talking about is a new slant in the heart and mind, a relevance demanded by our time. I believe the Christian message can roll with the punches and still come up the winner. We need to remember that our God is moving toward a purpose, and our fundamental task is to follow Him and the example of the apostle Paul who said, "To the Jews I became as a Jew, in order to win Jews; to those under the law I became as one under the law—though not being myself under the law—that I might win those under the law" (I Cor. 9:20).

I empathize with people who are homesick for the old ways. I know why some are reluctant to move from what was once considered a solid world to the upsetness of the contemporary scene. But God has put us here to work for Him, to train the new (and often enigmatic) generation to take over our tasks. We can turn to new ways and save many of them, or we can forsake them to

25

their unfortunate heritage, crawl into the shell of the past, and hold our ears and wait for the explosion.

You must make your own decision in this matter, but as for me, I want to be, to borrow a Youth for Christ slogan, "geared to the times, but anchored to the Rock!"

I had to learn to travel light—
to separate the musts *from the* wants.

4 COPING WITH TENSION

This subject focuses attention on three major mala-
dies of our time: tension, temper, and trouble. Any
physiologist will tell you we are putting abnormal strains
on our hearts, and I am referring now to the physical
organ, not the spirit.

I read an amusing story the other day. A housewife
had a nervous breakdown during a Sunday morning
church service. It came on when the choir was singing,
"Awake, my soul, stretch every nerve." That's what she
had been doing all week, stretching every nerve! That's
what her housework, shopping, the budget, the children,
the TV and radio commercials had been demanding of
her. Now, with the church pushing her to "stretch every
nerve"—well, that was too much!

May we not be paying too stiff an emotional price for
what we glibly refer to as "progress?" I can't make
myself believe the human body and nervous system was
designed for the sort of civilization man has cut out for
himself. They are tough, they can take an enormous
amount of strain, but there's a question as to how much
artificial stimuli, noise, speed, and prodding the body

can take. You have noticed, I am sure, that most radio and television commercials are more animated, more ear-splitting and nerve-racking than the programs they partition. Everything touted, from soap powder to stomach relief, is fast, fast, fast! How long can we operate as human beings under such artificial conditions?

Jesus told His disciples, "Do not be anxious for tomorrow, for tomorrow will take care of itself. . ." (Matt. 6:34). That's one way to slow down the adrenal gland. We had better learn this, because tensions won't decrease; they'll not become less, and whether we wish to face it or not, each of us has a breaking point. I have been surprised to see men and women whom I thought had everything under control, who seemed more than equal to any occasion, suddenly break down under the strain of responsibility. There are little storms raging inside of all of us, ministers and counsellors and psychologists included, that threaten to sweep us away if we don't call in the Master of wind and wave.

I have had personal lessons to learn in this area. I had to learn to travel light, to separate the "musts" from the "wants." I have always seen more things to do than I had energy to accomplish, so I had to reach the point where I discerned which things were supremely important and which were only relatively important. Then I programmed myself to the imperatives only. And do you know something? I discovered that at least 30 percent of the things I was doing were more energy-consuming than they were important.

I not only overextended myself for the day; I borrowed burdens from tomorrow. With nerves frayed and body and mind exhausted, it is small wonder I kept seeing collapse ahead. Anyone who adds the burdens of the future to those of the present is bait for a psycho ward! Something has to give.

I'm sure you've heard the story of the clock that

stopped suddenly one day. It had figured up how many times it had to tick in a year, more than 31 million times, so it just gave up. Then a fellow clock reminded it that it didn't have to tick them all at once, just one tick at a time.

That's what Jesus was getting at when He said, "Each day has enough trouble of its own," or, as the King James Version puts it, "Sufficient unto the day is the evil thereof."

John Henry Newman, an Anglican clergyman, was enroute back to England from a visit to Rome. The sailing ship upon which he was a passenger was becalmed between the islands of Corsica and Sardinia. It was June 16, 1833. Hours passed and the ship did not move. Newman, who had been under severe emotional stress, paced the deck, demanding of God that He send a wind to get them on their way. He even asked the captain if he couldn't do something to get things going! When night came and the ship's sail still hung motionless, Newman's patience broke. "Can't you do something?" he screamed at the captain. The captain replied quietly, "I am as anxious as you are to sail, but we who sail before the wind have learned to wait for it. We take one step at a time." Then, pointing to the sky, he said, "The star is shining again. If a wind rises tonight, we can chart our course by it."

Newman said, "You mean you can be guided by that one little star?" "Yes," replied the captain, "one needs the sun by day, but one little star is sufficient by night."

Suddenly Newman saw the light! "I've been looking for a sun to guide me," he said to a clergyman friend who was sailing with him, "and God has sent me a star. God dropped me here to teach me this lesson!" And in the inspiration of the moment and the glow of that experience, John Henry Newman wrote his greatest hymn:

Lead, kindly light! Amid the encircling gloom;
    Lead Thou me on.
The night is dark and I am far from home;
    Lead Thou me on!
Keep Thou my feet; I do not ask to see
The distant scene. One step enough for me.

One step at a time. Isn't that enough for anyone? "Sufficient for the day." That's great medicine for tension!

Of course we can't always do this in our own strength. One writer talks about "relaxing our souls in God," and that, of course, is the best way to do it. I've read books on how to relax, and some made me more tense than I was before! Psychologist Henry Link said his efforts to get his patients to calm down were unsuccessful until he began to tie in with his suggestions thoughts of God and words of the Bible. Now there is some danger in that: the Bible wasn't written to cure headaches or to be therapeutical. But I can assure you it helps to know we were made by and for God, that we belong to Him, and that because this is so, beneath all our restlessness are the strong and everlasting arms.

Tensions and temper are closely related. People who are chronically tired are usually chronically irritable. It is frightening to realize that in these days when the world is moving from one crisis to another, grave decisions are being made by men who are tired, jumpy, irritable. When one sees tempers flare among those who are electioneering, and in our legislative halls, he wonders how far men who so easily "blow their cool" can be trusted with the fate of millions of people.

How do we handle temper? For one thing, we don't ask God to take it away. Temper is power and we wouldn't be worth much without it. As one writer points out, "Temper is the driving force of life, the steam in the boiler that makes the wheels go round. The more vigorously tempered a man or woman is, the more potentially useful he is, and the better material in him." But he then goes on to point out that temper should just make the wheels turn, not burn out the bearings or blow off in the whistle!

Temper should be a driving, not a destroying force. Someone has written this verse about mishandled temper:

> When I have lost my temper
>> I have lost my reason, too.
> I'm never proud of anything
>> Which angrily I do.

> When I have talked in anger,
>> And my cheeks were flaming red,
> I have always uttered something
>> Which I wish I had not said.

> In anger I have never
>> Done a kindly deed or wise,
> But many things for which I felt
>> I should apologize.

> In looking back across my life,
>> And all I've lost or made,
> I can't recall a single time
>> When fury ever paid.

> So I struggle to be patient,
>> For I've reached a wiser age;
> I do not want to do a thing
>> Or speak a word in rage.

> I have learned from sad experience
>> That when my temper flies,
> I never do a worthy deed,
>> A decent deed, or wise.

Finally, a word about our third problem, trouble.

We all have a date with it sometime. It comes in many different forms: somebody slights you, lies about you, unjustly criticizes you, fails to give you due credit. Or someone you love gets off the beam morally and you have to carry his trouble with your own. There may be sickness, bereavement, financial disaster. "We can build machines to lift the strain of weariness from our muscles," says one writer, "but we can't build anything to lift the strain of trouble from our hearts."

Sometimes talking with someone who understands, who sympathizes or empathizes, will help. But usually we must go beyond human help to something deeper, and that "something deeper" is what Jesus was talking about in the upper room when He said, "Let not your heart be troubled; you believe in God, believe in me" (John 14:1).

Ah, here is the solution: something to believe in, and Someone who gives meaning to the struggle!

In my opinion, only those who can see purpose in suffering are the people of God. Although none of us knows fully what part the process has in fitting us for eternity, we know trouble fits us for both worlds. To Timothy Paul wrote, "If we suffer, we shall also reign with him. . ." (II Tim. 2:12). To the saints at Philippi he wrote, "For unto you it is given on behalf of Christ, not only to believe on him, but to suffer for his sake" (Phil. 1:29). To the Romans he wrote, "Tribulation worketh patience, and patience experience, and experience hope" (Rom. 5:3,4). And Jesus said, "In the world you shall have tribulation, but be of good cheer. . ." (John 16:33).

Are you hindered by tensions, temper, and trouble? Then synchronize your heartbeat with Christ's; grow steady and quiet in the knowledge that, if you are His by faith, you are sharing in some measure in the age-long cross and that you are a small but vital part in the healing, redeeming purposes of God!

Speech is a faithful gauge
of the condition of the heart.

5 THE PROBLEM OF IDLE WORDS

I once read that major recording companies hire people to do nothing but listen for flaws in newly cut
records, for any extraneous sounds or words which may
have been introduced inadvertently into the finished
product. Their sensitive ears are ever alert for anything
on the record that is not intended for public consump-
tion.

For example, I understand that recording artists have
been known to exclaim at the conclusion of a recording
session, "Boy, that was good!" not waiting for the
microphone to be turned off. Or perhaps an eccentric
bandleader, in a fit of anger, will break his baton over a
mike! Thus careful editing is a vital part of the recording
business.

Did you know the Bible says God is recording everything you and I say, good and bad? He employs no one
to "edit out" the embarrassing or condemning things we
say. "Every idle word that men shall speak," said our
Lord in Matthew 12:36, "they shall give an account
thereof in the day of judgment." If everything we have
ever said will be introduced as evidence against us in a

33

future day, it's a pretty frightening prospect, wouldn' you say?

Just what is an "idle" word? Not all Bible student agree on this. A man with whom I worked in the early days of my ministry thought any bit of humor was an idle word. He was against any playful interchange of words. Needless to say he was not only a very boring person, but he was as dry as sawdust in the pulpit!

There need be no speculation as to what Jesus mean by the word "idle." In this passage it is the Greek word *argos*, which means, simply, "unprofitable." It also means exactly what it implies in the English: idle, or "not working." The identical word is used in Matthew 20:3 where Jesus spoke of laborers "standing idle in th marketplace." They were free from work, unproductive So with "idle" words. They are "weeds in the garden patch of speech." They serve no good purpose.

It cannot be said that humorous words, per se (providing they are discreet and fitting), serve no good purpose. A sense of humor, the experts tell us, not only aid digestion, but in some cases prolongs life! People who see the bright and light side of life are always a delight to be with. One fruit of the Spirit is joy. Somehow I can't think of a joyous person as being a glum person. So "idle" words are not necessarily lighthearted words. On the other hand, dirty humor is definitely "a weed in th garden patch of speech."

Without the use of words, the business of life could not be carried on. Paul said it pleased God to save people by preaching, and preaching presupposes the employ ment of words, spoken words. Commerce would come to a dead stop without words. God wanted us to speak that's why He gave us the power of speech. But He also wants us to guard our words, to speak them with good purpose, not idly. Ungoverned, speech becomes a killed Robert Burton once said, "A blow with a word strike deeper than a blow with a sword." There are words th

34

an kindle everlasting animosities, words which can aughter reputations, words which degrade the mind, 'ords which incite to violence. Those are the words for hich men must give an account.

Just before Jesus made His statement concerning idle 'ords, a striking example had occurred. He had been isting out demons and the Pharisees, pressed for an xplanation, said He did so by the power of Beelzebub, ie prince of demons. It was a frivolous accusation, one hich Jesus dispatched in a sentence: Would Satan act gainst himself? The Pharisees must then have realized ow foolish, how unthinking, how idle was their accusaon. It was readily apparent that in their desperation to dict and slay Him, they spoke ill-advisedly, idly.

Solomon spoke often of the virtue of silence, suggestg that the more we say, the more apt we are to speak ly. More often than not the chain talker finds himself other people's business; he is more apt to slander, to ssip, than those who weigh their words. You may have ticed that the person whose mouth never stops or ws down is not infrequently a person who laces his nversation with profanity. It seldom fails that when an dividual's voice is heard booming out above everyone se's in a public place, that person is displaying a woeful ucity of thought and vocabulary, filling in the sizable ps with impieties. I never hear such a vociferous outuring of words but that my mind is drawn to Eccleistes 5:3, "A fool's voice is known by multitude of rds." Verbosity always increases the probability of traneous, weedy, idle words.

I suppose this is one reason Jesus' enemies continualplied Him with questions. They hoped to trip Him. hat solid proof of His deity it was that He never made . untrue statement or was guilty of a superfluity of rds! But the same cannot be said for us. The more ie talks, the greater the danger of putting one's foot in s mouth! James, who understood this danger so well,

35

wrote, "Let every one be quick to hear, slow to speak. . ." (James 1:19).

It has been said that a farmer need only hear, not see a wagon to know it is empty. The empty wagon makes more noise than the full one!

Why are idle words so serious? Because they reflect on God, on others, and on ourselves. Only man, of all God's creatures, has the gift of speech. That's because only he can reason, and it is by speech that he audibly expresses his thought processes. A parrot can be taught to speak, but he only parrots. He cannot reason. He would as soon swear before a minister as a sailor!

Thomas Edison was once introduced at a dinner as the inventor of the talking machine. "The gentleman who introduced me," said Edison, "should be corrected. God invented the talking machine. I only invented the first one that can be shut off!" Well, God did indeed invent the "talking machine," giving it (man) the gift of vocal expression. To abuse this unique privilege is to be held forever accountable.

A person's accent often betrays his national or geographical origin. We can tell an Englishman, or a Canadian, or a German, by the peculiarities of his accent. Now just as an accent tells us where a person is from, so his speech is a faithful gauge of the condition of his heart. Spurgeon once said, "What lies in the well of the heart will come up in the bucket of speech." Jesus said the same thing but phrased it differently, "Out of the abundance of the heart the mouth speaketh" (Matt 12:34).

A man once said to me, "I'm afraid I do swear now and then, but only when I'm mad." He may have considered this an excuse. But it's what we say when we are off guard that reveals the true condition of the heart. God has no categories in this respect; He doesn't overlook words spoken in anger and punish those spoken deliberately. "For by thy words [all words] thou shalt

stified," He said in Matthew 12:37, "and by thy
ords thou shalt be condemned." Actually, it is not so
uch that our words condemn us as that our words
veal whether we are justified or condemned.

During the days of the Spanish Inquisition a man was
ought before an inquisitorial body and examined as to
s acceptance of the doctrines of the church. He was
sured he could speak freely, that nothing he said
uld be held against him. But when he paused for a
oment in his testimony, he heard the scratching of a
n behind a curtain. Someone had been writing down
erything he said!

A popular Negro spiritual bears the title, "My God's
Vriting All the Time." That's good theology. Record-
s are relatively new to man, but God has been listening
d recording from the time man fell in the Garden.
evelation 20:12 envisions a day when every idle word
ll be played back. "And the books," wrote John,
vere opened."

I have heard people say, "I've never done anything
n ashamed of." Anyone who would tell a whopper like
at would be likely to also say, "I've never said any-
ing I'm ashamed of." But who of us would like to hear
ayed back every word we have uttered this past year?
re you say there would be no blushes, no apologies,
regrets? What temerity would be required to even
tertain the idea that many of our words are not hasty,
chosen, and sometimes vicious!

Until recently the press was not allowed to quote the
esident of the United States verbatim, but there have
ver been any such restrictions on God. Men will be
oted in the Judgment word for word.

When I was a young man there was a popular broad-
ster in the Chicago area who had a daily children's
ogram. One day, when he had concluded the broadcast
d thought the engineer had shut off his microphone,
said, as he gathered up his script, "That ought to hold

37

you little so-and-so's." But his mike had not been turned off and his vulgar impropriety went out over the air. The damage had been done; there was no way to recall his words. He was fired on the spot, and a long and successful children's program came to an abrupt and sad end.

God's "mike" is never off. All words, unforgiven by Christ and by our fellow men against whom we have uttered them, will demand accountability. How fitting then, to pray with the psalmist: "Set a watch, O Lord before my mouth; keep the door of my lips" (Ps. 141:3).

Nothing is easier to do
than to criticize in others
the weaknesses we don't have!

6 DON'T JUDGE

It was Byron J. Langenfeld who said, "Rare is the person who can weigh the faults of others without putting his thumb on the scales." Because man is so often lacking in data and biased in his opinion of others, Jesus was obliged to deal with this sin in His Sermon on the Mount: "Judge not, that you be not judged," He warned. "For with what judgment you judge, you shall be judged; and with what measure you mete, it shall be measured to you again" (Matt. 7:1).

The term *Christian cruelty* may be a misnomer, but some of you know what I mean. There is a type of cruelty practiced by some who wear the Christian label that is nothing less than downright devilishness and destructiveness.

I refer to the sin of judging.

Now I know many people defend evil in their lives and in the lives of others by throwing up what they consider the perfect defense, "Judge not, that you be not judged!" Didn't Jesus Himself say that? And doesn't it mean that we are never to weigh a person by his deeds?

No, that isn't exactly what Jesus meant when H[e] warned against judging others. What He was referring t[o] was the careless formation of an opinion with respect t[o] others' *motives*. This squares with Webster's definition "To criticize or censure; to *think* or *suppose*."

If we see a man reel out of a bar and stagger down th[e] street, it is not "judging" to say he is intoxicated[.] Judging is jumping at *unverified conclusions*; it is relat[-] ing as fact that which is only hearsay or conjecture. It i[s] reading evil into another's motives merely because i[t] seems "obvious." It is this that Jesus scorned when H[e] said, "Judge not." He was condemning the common ac[t] of appointing oneself a committee of one to be the judg[e] and jury in matters concerning which only partial knowl[-] edge or evidence is available.

I want to cite four reasons why this is dangerou[s] business and should be carefully avoided by those wh[o] wish to prevent this sin from becoming part and parc[el] of their lives.

First, we should not judge because we cannot alway[s] believe our eyes and ears.

Oh, of course anything *we* pass along is absolutel[y] authentic! Aunt Agatha could not possibly have bee[n] wrong, for she knew personally the lady who got [it] firsthand from her husband who works with the ma[n] whose cousin knew it to be a fact! How much mo[re] authentic can you get?

Have you ever played the parlor game called "Go[s]- sip?" The players form a line, then the person at th[e] head of the line whispers a sentence into the ear of th[e] one next to him, who in turn whispers what he thoug[ht] he heard to the one next to him, and so on down th[e] line. When the statement gets to the end of the line, an[y] similarity to its original form is purely coincidental!

This kind of "gossip" is fun, but the real kind isn'[t.] Far too often it may strike down the reputation of a[n] innocent person. Such stories are like feathers tossed into the wind. They can never be recovered.

Second, we should not judge because things are not always as they appear. We do not always understand what we see. Let me cite a case in point.

A pastor in a small Illinois town was seen leaving a tavern at 12:45 A.M. "He was with another man, and both were drunk," swore the informant.

When confronted with the accusation, the minister readily admitted that he had left the tavern with another man at that late hour, but it was not like it seemed. He, at the request of a distraught wife, had entered the bar to persuade the husband, who was squandering his paycheck, to go home. His efforts met with success at precisely 12:45 A.M., at which time they both left the tavern. Of course the minister had not been drinking. He stumbled while trying to hold the intoxicated husband upright.

But the story, with all its lurid implications, would not die. It grew and spread out of all proportion in that small town. The minister's deacons upbraided him for what they considered an indiscretion, and finally the man was dismissed from his church.

This exemplifies the "Christian cruelty" to which I earlier alluded. Only heaven could have a book large enough to record the "casualties" of this kind, men and women who have fallen beneath cruel fusillades fired from deadly "gossip guns."

I once had a similar experience when I was a young pastor in my second church. Some of my no-punches-pulled sermons got to certain families in the church, and in the course of time they set a trap for me, one tailor-made for my inexperience and youthful naivete.

Being anxious to settle any misunderstandings, I agreed to meet with three of the unhappy families in one of their homes; the purpose, as far as I was concerned, being to pour oil on the troubled waters. In retrospect I am amazed that anyone could have been as incredibly unsophisticated as I was. I was alone among six antagonists, with not even one friendly witness.

The result of that meeting was that everything I said was twisted, taken completely out of context, and then published abroad. Had it not been for the substantial number of church members who trusted me and knew them, I would undoubtedly have been unceremoniously ousted.

Jesus said the devil is a liar and the father of lies (John 8:44). Bear that in mind whenever you are tempted to repeat or pass along a rumor, or even a fact, that might damage another or adversely affect their whole life.

Third, we should not judge because we may be setting our own standards and judging others by them.

We all have a strong tendency to formulate our own personal criteria for proper Christian conduct, then measure everyone by them. If someone fails to meet these standards we are apt to demean them.

Radio ministers are probably more familiar with this type of brutal censure than others, for we reach such a variety of people and cover such a broad cross-section of the nation. On any given day I speak to people who hold literally dozens of different doctrinal positions and interpret the Bible in manifold ways. It has been interesting to note through the years how a certain message will draw the highest praise from some and the bitterest criticism from others. I can empathize with the political candidates. They can't win in hostile territory!

Another disturbing person is the one who is always alert for statements and viewpoints which differ from his own. Such people can seldom resist "lowering the boom" in a letter. I have known people to liberally support and to highly recommend my broadcast over a period of years, only to suddenly become an enemy because they disagreed with something that I said. "Take me off your mailing list," they write. "I'll never send you another dollar." Because I transgressed their personal opinion, I was no longer a friend or a counselor.

I remember how this worked a few years ago when I changed the format of my program in an effort to attract those who normally will not listen to a religious broadcast. A number of innovations were made with this in mind but the reaction was immediate, and far from heartening. Although no compromise with the gospel was involved, many wrote to say they would no longer support or listen to the program. They had set up their own private concept of how a gospel broadcast should be conducted and were judging me by those standards. Cruelly and inaccurately, I was being accused of "no longer preaching the gospel." I also remember the time we published a picture of Mrs. Jess wearing earrings. That brought a storm of protest from some of the dear sisters. Mrs. Jess was accused of being "worldly," of being a "poor testimony." Two of the criticizers, to my personal knowledge, were unable to win their husbands to the Lord; yet they were on a perpetual snoop for jewelry, short hair, makeup, and other things they considered sinful. They were well trained in trivia.

Fourth, we should not judge because we may not understand the weaknesses and battles of others.

Nothing is easier to do than to criticize in others weaknesses we don't have, or that do not tempt us. Like the 90-year-old woman who was heard to say in a croaking voice, "I can't understand people who call themselves Christians and still want to dance. That's no temptation to me!" Well, I would think not! We see only people's failures, not the hundreds of battles they win. Perhaps if we could see their hearts, as God does, we would realize what struggles those victories represented. David was a man after God's own heart, not because he was sinless but because he wanted to do right, and because when he sinned he was thoroughly repentant.

43

I can't tell you why some people struggle a lifetime with certain weaknesses while others are immediately delivered at conversion. I do know many things are involved: heredity, environment, genetic makeup, even prenatal influences. But I believe Christians should make it a point to be sympathetic and longsuffering, remembering Paul's admonition to the Galatians: "Even if a man should be detected in some sin, my brothers, the spiritual ones among you should quietly set him back on the right path, not with any feeling of superiority, but being yourselves on guard against temptation" (6:1, *Phillips*).

My plea is not that we condone sin, but that we be charitable and reticent to condemn others, since we may be guilty ourselves of infractions as bad or worse in God's eyes. Let us strive to adhere to Paul's admonition to Timothy, "Be thou an example of the believers in word, in conversation, in charity, in faith, in purity" (I Tim.4:12).

Each of us casts some kind of shadow,
one that will have a
decisive influence on others.

7 THE PROBLEM OF SHADOWS

As children we learned the little rhyme:

> I have a little shadow
> That goes in and out with me,
> And what can be the use of him
> Is more than I can see.

Of what use is a shadow? "It's an escape from the sun's heat," you might say, but if you·were a Brahman in India you would throw away your food if the shadow of a lower caste person passed over it. On the other hand, when Mahatma Ghandi was living, many of his admiring countrymen would try to place themselves in his shadow, slight as it was, in the belief that a spiritual or material blessing would come to them.

Luke records in Acts 5 that afflicted people pressed close to Peter in the hope his shadow would fall on them and they would be healed. Some say this was only superstition, that there actually was no healing power in Peter's shadow, but there is no suggestion in the text that this was not an actual supernatural occurrence. We remember Jesus used means other than His personal touch. A woman was healed when she touched His garment. A blind man was healed with clay Jesus placed on his eyes. Why not believe that He could use even Peter's shadow to heal the afflicted?

I would like to emphasize the fact that each of us casts some kind of a shadow, one that will have a decisive influence on others. Influence is as impossible to disown or escape as a shadow. Like a stone cast into a pool creates ripples that widen until they touch the shore, so none of us can exist in any sphere of life without causing ripples of influence that widen until they "touch the shores of infinity."

We don't think about that as often as we should. We say we are too unimportant to lay hold on other people's lives, to shape anyone else's thoughts or mold their opinions; too unimportant to inspire or depress anyone. That, however, is not true. The shadow of our lives invariably falls across the lives of others. There is an invisible pull that, although we may be unaware of it, is there nonetheless.

What is a fad but something one person starts and others follow? It may be long or short hair, long or short skirts, dirty blue jeans and white shoes, or chain letters. It amuses me when young people think they are resisting convention when they dress in weird costumes and lose their faces in hair. They may not be mimicking their elders, but they are mimicking their peers! When Castro and his buddy, Che Guevara, popularized this beard business it was a badge of rebellion. Not everyone who wears a beard now is rebellious, obviously, but the fad began in that shadow.

Often the matter of shadow-casting gets into the serious matter of moral choice. Remember in John's gospel, chapter 21, where disgusted and discouraged Peter said, "I go a-fishing"? He meant he was through, he had "had it," and was returning to his former business profession. That shadow fell across the other disciples, and they said, "We also go with thee" (v.3). Here Peter's shadow was not one of healing!

I have seen one man, by his corrosive influence, break the morale of a business or of a whole church. He gets off the beam and others follow. I know of so many good churches that have been split because someone, with a personal bone to pick, pulled out and took many others with him. I am not implying that leaving a church is always wrong. Sometimes it is a matter of principle, in which case those who stay and support a charlatan pastor, or a liberal message, are casting shadows which could well have spiritually disastrous results.

I remember a church I pastored as a young man. It had been supporting financially a denomination laced with liberal theologians and causes, and I had strong convictions that this support should cease. But some of the good diehards in the membership thought we should not make waves and incur the displeasure of the denominational hierarchy. Although some privately acknowledged the inconsistency of supporting enemies of the gospel, in the church business meetings they vigorously opposed any change. The weak arguments of these sincere but spiritually insensitive people influenced nearly half of the church members to continue their compromise position. These were not vicious people; many, I am sure, were Christians. But they cast a shadow which has since been instrumental in channeling thousands of dollars into an organization that not only tolerates, but elevates, theological renegades.

As I have thought about this in subsequent years, I have concluded that the influence of a shadow is always positive, never neutral. We may believe we are neutral but our influence never is: it votes either yes or no. "He that is not with me is against me," Jesus said (Matt. 12:30). Someone has said, "Not to choose is itself a choice." When we straddle moral or spiritual issues, that shadow always affects others in a positive way.

47

Influence is often subtle, even unconscious, but wield it we do, however unintentional. Let us suppose a husband and wife come to the realization when their children are teenagers that they haven't been setting a very good example. They haven't spent enough time with them. They have lost some communication. They have been neglecting the church. Talking it over, they say, "We'd better begin having a good influence on the kids. We should start talking with them, going to church. We should tell them how important it is to be honest and moral and religious." So they call the children in and go over their list, point by point, after which they feel a great sense of relief. They have influenced their children!

But what about the bygone years of unconscious influence? Can those be remedied or erased with a chummy little talk, a lecture, a few apologies for past indifference? No, the shadows of those parents have fallen across the lives of their children since they were babies! Heartbroken parents tell me they have lost their children to the world, to the hippie community, to liberalism. Now they want to know what they can do. Some confess they became concerned only after their sons or daughters were in college. Well, now it's too late, Mom and Dad! I'm sorry. The horse is out of the barn.

I sat in a restaurant the other day and heard two boys in the next booth using unbelievably bad language. I judge they were in their early teens. My initial impulse was to give them a good talking to, but then I thought that these boys ever since they were small children have probably lived in the shadow of profanity, hearing it first from their parents and being exposed to it constantly on the screen. I decided it was the mouths of some much older people that needed to be washed out with soap!

As a father I would rather die than have a child of mine hear me swear, or tell a dirty story, or say anything that would undermine his confidence in me, in God, in the gospel, or in the church. A child's attitude toward his school, his church, and his country is often determined by casual conversations around the table. He is also adversely affected by such things as knowing that his parents cheat on their income tax, or lie about their children's ages, or break traffic laws when no policemen are around.

It has been well said:

If a child lives with hostility, he learns to fight.
If he lives with criticism, he learns to condemn.
If he lives with fear, he learns to be apprehensive.
If he lives with jealousy, he learns to hate.
If he lives with self-pity, he learns to be sorry for himself.
If he lives with acceptance, he learns to love.
If he lives with fairness, he learns justice.
If he lives with honesty, he learns what truth is.
If a child lives with friendliness, he learns that the world is a nice place in which to live.

Lastly, shadows cast an immortal influence, one that lives long beyond the life from which it emanated. Death never destroys a shadow; it never stops influence. Many years ago infidel Robert Ingersoll wrote a terrible book in which he set forth superficial arguments against the Bible and Christianity. That black shadow still falls across people's lives, making skeptics of some who never saw him, but who believe him.

By way of contrast, I'm thinking of the many books which have influenced my life for God, many written by men now gone. The apostle Paul is still influencing people to believe in Christ with words he wrote on papyrus in a Roman prison.

One writer, speaking of influence, says: "A man may have lived a thousand years ago and died unknown, but he struck a little blow on the wires of human solidarity that will tremble on to the end of time." It is this force, by the way, that Jesus chose to evangelize the world: witnessing and influencing, the pull of one life upon another.

How long is your shadow? And what is it doing and saying? Remember, once exerted it can never be recalled. You may change, but the influence of former days will go on. It will not change with you!

Recall with me these sobering words of the apostle Paul to the Thessalonians: "For you yourselves know how you ought to follow our example; because we did not act in an undisciplined manner among you . . . in order to offer ourselves as a model for you, that you might follow our example" (II Thess. 3:7,9 *NAS*).

We get uptight over current events
because we have an improper perspective
of time and history.

8 THE QUEST FOR TRANQUILITY

No strong, weighty argument is needed to convince us that we live in extremely tense times and that everyone is seeking a measure of inner stability. The past decade has seen an intensification of every major problem: crime, racial bias, war, dehumanization in virtually every area of life. Society is shot through with fear and confusion and we had best steel ourselves for more of the same, for we will undoubtedly live out our days in troublous and anxious times.

As Dr. Elton Trueblood has aptly said, "Whatever the course of history may be in the next years, it will not be a course of tranquility." He may have been thinking of the fact that in the twenty-seven years since 1945 there have been fifty-five wars of significant size, duration, and intensity throughout the world. Wars continue to rage in Southeast Asia, the Middle East is a tinderbox, Russia and China growl at each other across their borders, and many analysts see in these and other tension points the possible triggering of an Armageddon.

We cannot hope for anything resembling permanent peace when nations have sharply conflicting ideologies and when the two mightiest nations have stockpiled enough nuclear weapons to kill all mankind many times over; when the nuclear warhead on a modern missile can spread atomic fires over an area 150 times greater than that which burned at Hiroshima! A single Polaris-type missile is capable of killing millions of people outright, while millions more would die from smoke, dust, falling debris, and radioactive fallout.

It is therefore quite natural, while living under the sword of Damoclese, to be restless, even panicky. We know, as one writer points out, that peace in our time is as unlikely as was prosperity in the South immediately after the Civil War, because the conditions for peace do not exist. "We are in the monsoon," he added, "and we must weather it out."

What an ideal time this is for Christians to look to Isaiah's formula for inner poise in a time of crisis. "In quietness and in confidence" he wrote, "shall be your strength" (30:15). Quietness and confidence! How the world needs that! What an essential ingredient in the hour of mind-boggling, nerve-racking strain!

You and I have the opportunity, as no other generation before us, to let the solidity and comfort of the Bible come alive to us and through us. When the Bible speaks of inner peace, as it often does, it is talking about a spiritual achievement, not mere placidity. This latter might be the result of laziness, mental dullness, or possibly low blood pressure! What we need, and what God wants us to have, is the ability to maintain dignity, calm, and rationality in the midst of ever-increasing strain and global peril.

One reason we get uptight over current events is that we have an improper perspective of time and history. We stand so close to ourselves we can't see the overall plan and situation. Once the psalmist looked so important to himself he thought he was the world, but then he looked again and saw himself against the background of a much larger point of reference and expressed his new viewpoint with this resolve, "I will lift up mine eyes unto the hills" (Ps. 121:1). You see, it steadied him to look at something big, solid, and enduring. That is what history should do for us. We don't know how long man has been on this planet. The guesstimates range from thousands to millions of years but whichever, no major or minor tragedies, personal or global, have stopped or slowed the wheels, or in any way thwarted God's plan for the ages. Some of us who have lived through a number of presidential elections have felt at the time that if a certain man were elected to that office it would mean the end of the world, or at least the end of America. But some of those men have been elected, and on we go, with God still at the helm of human affairs. I believe in trying to change my community, my nation, and the world because all are in bad shape, but I am sure it would displease God if my concern gave me ulcers, or high blood pressure, or sent me to a premature grave.

Too often we Christians forget that God, not Mao Tse-tung or Kosygin or Nixon, is running this world. Actually, nothing of world-shaking importance rests on any one human being. Any one of us could drop out of the race tonight and we would be missed by only a handful. I know it is hard to look at life like that. If we stand too close to it, a six-foot grave can fill the whole earth. We can allow small annoyances in our social contacts or our home life to become mountains that blot out the sky. But let's not move the world into our living rooms; let's not imagine the events of our times are altogether unique, that nothing like them has ever happened before. A good remedy for self-centeredness is to read the obituary columns of the newspaper. Every day thousands of people are moving out of this earthly realm, but life goes right on. The wheels won't stop when your heart, or mine, does. This world is very old.

It has had a good many crises before we were born and there will be more after we are gone. Don't try to brace yourself against them all. Learn to roll with the punches!

I am not suggesting that we live carelessly or recklessly, telling ourselves we don't count, but rather to look at things in their proper perspective, to "believe what the centuries say against the hours," as Emerson put it. Don't be less than God wants you to be but don't try to be the whole human race either!

"In quietness and confidence shall be your strength," said Isaiah. To be quiet and confident one must have emotional balance. Now emotions are fine. They are necessary driving forces but they can destroy us if they get out of hand. Unfortunately, this is what is happening on many fronts. People are shouting at each other, often without regard for accuracy or reason. Someone has said this is the "United Hates of America." I am afraid that's at least partially true. We can't avoid seeing it: class against class, black against white, young people against their elders. And what is even more incongruous and embarrassing is that some professing Christians, even some nationally known preachers, are in the forefront of the shouting match!

It has always been my conviction that we Christians were put here to be a healing influence in society. If we can't take the heat out of the hysteria, if we can't reduce the fever, what good are we? The very last thing we should allow ourselves is the dubious "luxury" of runaway emotion. Under no circumstances should we let our mouths run faster than our minds. Someone has pointed out that "the more we run out of ideas the louder we are likely to shout." I think of the preacher who wrote at one point in his sermon manuscript, "Argument weak here—wave arms and yell like the devil!" Well, isn't it true, the weaker the argument, the louder we are likely to shout?

The Christian who, through prayer, commitment, and

the yielding of his members to Christ, finds the strength (not the weakness) of quietness and confidence, will have control over his emotions. Now I know from personal experience this is a big job. I have many inner conflicts. As one writer put it, "Part of us is heading north and the rest of us is heading south." But let us make it a major goal of our lives to get our clamorous selves into some sort of balance. This is not to suggest cowlike placidity. We are not vegetables. But just as the equilibrium of the earth is held in balance by the pull of two strong forces against each other, so the Christian can be lighthearted without being sentimental, serious without being sad, and concerned without being a crackpot. It's all right to raise an eyebrow, but not the roof!

Nothing gives the heart peace, the step steadiness, and the soul tranquility like the assurance that we are standing on solid ground; that the present as well as the future belongs to God; and that above all we can afford to wait.

I believe God is a good God. If I didn't, I wouldn't believe the Bible, or sacred history, or my own experience. I must believe that whatever happens to me is for my own good, and that whatever happens to the world, God has wisely allowed it to happen. I have asked Him to direct my life, not to make it easy. And if I don't believe He will, when as His son I have asked Him to do so, I can't believe in Him at all.

Suppose my daughter came to me and said, "Dad, I want to do everything to make you happy. I know you've had a lot more experience than I and that I can avoid a lot of mistakes and heartaches if I follow your advice. Please guide me, and I'll do my best to abide by your suggestions."

What would I do? Decide that because she had put herself completely in my hands that I would do everything possible to make her miserable, confused, and awkward? What parent would do that?

I have asked God to run my life. I have told Him I

love Him and respect His judgment, that He knows all things and I know scarcely anything. Do you think He will foul everything up for me, or allow someone else, or some circumstances to do so? Not on your tintype! He will see that I am useful to Him, and that I make it through all the confusion and mix-ups safely.

And if you ask Him, He'll do the same for you!

> I cannot see the way I go;
>   I go not knowing why;
> But this I know, each step is set
>   By Him who is Most High!
> And so I gladly tread His path,
>   Nor fear whate'er betide,
> Assured that when I win His smile,
>   I shall be satisfied.

If human reluctance can be broken down
by sheer persistence,
how much more can we count on
God's great willingness?

9 DOES IT PAY TO PRAY?

Some years ago a British scientist decided to settle, via the "scientific method," whether prayer served any purpose. His question: Are the people most prayed for any different from others?

He deduced that the most prayed for people were members of the royal family and children of the clergy, therefore they should be healthier, happier, and longer-lived than anyone else. But it turned out that they weren't, therefore he announced that he had proved "scientifically" that prayer was useless and impractical.

It was obvious, however, that the man didn't understand prayer or its qualifications. Still he was probably as well informed as some Christians on the subject. I bump into people all the time who have soured on prayer because they think it is a magic lamp to be rubbed. When no genie appears, they become disillusioned. They pray for better health and remain ill. They pray for a sick loved one and he or she dies. Parents pray for the safety of their sons on the battlefield—but still they get "the telegram."

So why pray?

Almost everyone, at one time or another, has considered prayer some sort of a magic cure. We like to think it manipulates God, that it causes Him to do something He has no intention of doing otherwise; something He may even be reluctant to do. People pray for certain things, then when answers don't drop down out of the sky or come to pass tomorrow, they give up. Prayer, to them, is like dropping a coin in a slot machine. If they don't hit the jackpot the first time, they surrender to a sense of futility.

I don't profess to understand why, but God wants us to pray with importunity. This, according to the dictionary definition, is "stubborn persistence." I confess I have some personal problems with this. I've been tempted to say, "God knows my needs. Why pester Him with them?" But that isn't the story Jesus had to tell. In Luke 11, He related the parable of the importunate man who knocked on his friend's door at midnight to ask for three loaves of bread to feed an unexpected guest. The sleepy man told him to go away, but eventually he became weary with the ceaseless knocking and gave in. That's a simple story, but I believe it has very wide implications.

I guess you could say that, in a way, this man answered his own prayer. Caught in a bind, he had two alternatives; he could pray for God to send him bread, or he could go to his neighbor's house and ask for some. Apparently the latter was much quicker.

But there is more to the story. Even when he arrived at the source of supply, it wasn't easy to obtain. His sleepy neighbor didn't give in easily. He not only had to make the journey to the neighbor's house; he had to stay outside and plead at some length for the fulfillment of his need. He got what he came after, but in the process he learned persistence and patience. I think that is what Jesus was trying to teach concerning prayer. He wants us to strengthen the muscles of the heart and mind.

I am confident that we often ask God to do things for

us which we are capable of doing for ourselves. As an example, many of us are deeply concerned about the pornographic material that is flooding our nation, also the sometimes sensuous fare offered on television. We are concerned because we know this sort of thing breeds crime, violence, and immorality. So what do we do? Mostly, we pray that God will do something to turn it off. But so far He hasn't reached down and destroyed these lewd institutions or cracked the skulls of their owners. He has, instead, provided those who know how to combat these perils in the courts.

It is sometimes possible to answer our own prayers. Other people are sometimes more responsive than we may think they are. You might be surprised what a well written, unimpassioned letter to your senator or congressman will do to influence legislation. You might also be surprised what a letter to a radio or television station, or a newspaper, can do. Most people are reasonable and when they encounter resistance they may move in the opposite direction. The very minute percentage of protesters in this country have learned this; that's why they accomplish so much and even influence men in the highest governmental offices. They may not be patient, but they are persistent. God wants us to be both when we pray.

I am personally responsive to the ideas and requests of others. Many letters of constructive criticism make an impression on me and are often the means of improvements in my ministry. I may not always write and thank the critic, but if the criticism makes sense, if I feel it comes from a responsible person who is not filled with hate, I accept it and profit from it. I believe most people are like this. None of us are so smart that we can't learn and continue learning.

Sometimes we can answer our own prayers through communication with others. For example, suppose you have had a falling out with another member of your church, or a neighbor, or a member of your family. Don't pray for a reconciliation until you have made every effort, on a personal basis, to resolve your differences. When a Christian wife tells me she is praying for her unsaved husband's conversion, but does so with a note of bitterness and hopelessness in her voice, I doubt that she will ever see her efforts rewarded. Often we pray for people we cannot personally contact, but if they live in our own home, or our own city, then we should put feet on our prayers. To pray for a member of the family, then snap his head off in conversation a dozen times a day, is an exercise in futility. As often as not we can answer our own prayers with Christian courtesy and unselfishness.

But returning now to Jesus' parable of the importunate host and his sleepy neighbor: here we are told what to do when prayer seems useless, when our cries seem to go unheeded and to make no difference. The formula is simple and clear: keep on praying! Luke 18:1: "Men ought always to pray, and not faint [lose heart]." This is not because God delights in seeing us squirm and plead, but because He first wants to test our sincerity, and second, because the longer we pray about something the more objective may be our prayers. I have found that sometimes when I pray about something long, often I later discover that it wasn't important after all and I was better off without it.

Yet the story goes deeper than that. It shows us that if a friend can be coaxed out of bed at midnight to do us a good turn, God is much more sensitive and willing than he is. As one writer states it, "If human reluctance can be broken down by sheer persistence, how much more can we count on God's great willingness?"

Ethel Romig Fuller has written this meaningful verse:

If radio's slim fingers can pluck a melody
From the night—and toss it over a continent or sea;

If the petalled white notes of a violin
Are blown across the mountains or the city's sin;
If songs, like crimson roses, are culled from thin blue air
Why should we mortals wonder if God answers prayer?

Jesus said, "If you then, who are evil, know how to give good gifts to your children, how much more will your Father who is in heaven give good things to those who ask him?" (Matt. 7:11, *RSV*).

I once had a neighbor who was anything but a Christian. I saw no evidence in his life that he loved God or knew Jesus Christ, yet Christmas day his children were loaded down with toys that I knew cost him more than he could afford. An evil man giving his children good gifts! How much more willing is our heavenly Father to give His children what they request? "How much more," said Jesus, "shall your heavenly Father give good gifts to those who ask him?" I don't believe our problem is as much unanswered prayer as it is unoffered prayer!

Now it's a mistake to think that prayer is a fitting substitute for an education, for work, or for discipline of mind. In fact, prayer works best when we work. Yet I would not minimize God's willingness and responsiveness. If prayer is ineffective, it is usually our unwillingness to knock and keep knocking, to ask and keep asking.

People say, "I can't pray because God isn't real to me." They should say, "God isn't real to me because I don't pray!" I have never come across a "prayer warrior" to whom God was not intensely real. Such have found that prayer not only changes things; they have also found that it changes pray-ers.

In recent years there has been a lot of silly talk about the "death" of God. It is said that God is "eclipsed," that if He is there He doesn't care. Men say they are waiting for God to "come alive." Well, has it ever occurred to them that God is waiting for them to come alive? If we want Him to answer our prayers we had better first answer His!

John Heuss refers to prayer as a two-way street in the following lines:

> Prayer is neither black magic nor is it a form of demand. Prayer is a relationship. The act of praying is more analogous to clearing away the underbrush which shuts out a view than it is to begging in the street.

> Yet all prayer has one basic purpose. We pray not to get something, but to open up a two-way street between us and God, so that we and others may inwardly become something.

God will never cease to extract from our lives
the gold that demonstrates to the world
what trials can do to enhance those
marked for His Distinguished Service medal.

10 SUFFERING CAN BE GOLDEN

Some time ago I came across a little proverb which, like so many of those authored by man, has only an element of truth in it. "Suffering is sin's index finger," it went, "pointing out something wrong."

That this is sometimes true, no one can validly deny. But to assume that suffering is invariably the result of evil in our lives is not only refuted by experience and observation; it is also repudiated by Scripture. A far better maxim is this one: "To have suffered much is like knowing many languages: it gives the sufferer access to many more people."

Unquestionably, suffering has from the dawn of creation been a frustrating human problem. It can have a variety of consequences, depending on our understanding (or misunderstanding) of it. Many have turned completely from God because of their own suffering, or the suffering of others; they have renounced all faith in God and divine providence. Others have become cynical, even agnostic, in their view of life because of it. Suffering has mellowed, sweetened and refined many under its white-hot heat. As in so many other things, it is not suffering, per se, that is to be judged by the results it produces.

Men are especially perplexed by the sufferings of "good" people, people who have seemingly done nothing to "deserve" adversity. They have never stolen anything, never been unkind to anyone, never knowingly trespassed on another's rights. Yet it is commonly known that many such people languish beneath perpetual heartaches and physical debilities, while many renowned culprits appear to thrive physically, emotionally, financially, and socially. Those who assume that justice is meted out in this life or not at all will understandably question the reality of a loving and just God. Indeed, without an ultimate evening of scores by a final, all-inclusive judgment, as promised in the Bible, life is admittedly a house of horrors in which the meek inherit nothing and the strong gain everything!

If he is to keep from being inundated by emotional frustration, the Christian must keep his faith sharply whetted on an unswerving belief in the absolute sovereignty of God and the eventual righting of all wrongs, together with the punishment of all unforgiven evil. This is not easy, for we are naturally ignorant about many things. God's purposes are often obscured. The most common reaction to adversity is, "What have I done to deserve this?" Unless we carefully read, and unflinchingly believe, the many Scriptural warnings about the certainty of, the need for, and the salutary effects of testing, we will be left without any suitable answer to the problem of suffering. We will then have to agree with the skeptic who insists life is a gigantic accident, that it is a game of chess in which men are pawns of the uncertain, impersonal Hand of Destiny.

The classic example of a man who had grave doubts about God's goodness, but who eventually emerged from his grueling trials with rejuvenated and sharpened faith, is Job. After his Gethsemane he said, "But he knoweth the way that I take: when he hath tried me, I shall come forth as gold" (Job 23:10).

Job learned, as most of us do at some period of life, that there are faults, failures, and evil tendencies which need subduing or eradicating, weaknesses which require extreme corrective measures, if they are to be prevented from partially or wholly destroying us. Many years ago I saw men using flame throwers in the South to destroy weeds in cotton fields. They may now use other methods, but I remember how deftly those flame throwers were handled. In awkward hands they would no doubt have destroyed the cotton crop.

The longer I live the more convinced I become that God's Spirit acts in our lives in much the same way as those flame throwers were used to rid the cotton fields of weeds. There are weeds in your life and mine that need to be destroyed that the fruit of the Spirit may grow. I would also assume that the more potentially valuable the crop, the more often the flame throwers would be used.

I know this is a crude illustration, but the analogy comes to me as I observe the testings to which so many Christians, so many "good" people, are subjected. It is patently true that in most cases the deeper one's dedication to the Person and will of God, the more intense are the dross-removing fires. Nor need any feel that when he has reached a certain stage of Christian maturity the heat will be lessened, or no longer applied. Because we are human, there will always be impurities in our lives, so when God comes across some gold-bearing ore in us that is especially promising, He will never cease to extract from it the gold He needs to honor His name and to demonstrate to the world what trials can do to enhance the lives of those marked for His Distinguished Service medal.

Many Christians dread periods of testing instead of welcoming them as they should. We should know beforehand that He will never bend us to the breaking point. You and I might break under the apostle Paul's load, so that's undoubtedly the reason we have never experienced it. Yet we have God's solemn promise that He "will not suffer us to be tempted [Gr., *peiraze,* tried, tested] above that we are able ... to bear" (I Cor. 10:13). This means some people can stand hotter fires than others.

I remember that some years ago my wife and I were going through a period of testing more severe than we had ever known before, or have known since. Both of us were nearly crushed beneath a burden of sorrow and frustration. Wendell Loveless, who was our pastor at the time, said to us, "God would never subject any of His children to such a test if He didn't trust them implicitly and love them deeply." This was a great encouragement to us, although it was not until a much later date that God lifted the burden.

Since then I have had many occasions to share our experience with others, and I believe it helped them bear their burdens. As Christians, we must find the place of commitment where we will acknowledge, not just with our lips, but in our hearts, that God knows the future as well as the past, and is therefore able to gauge to the most expert degree the ability each of us has to bear burdens and to benefit by them. If I didn't believe God was able to safeguard my spiritual interests, I could never accept Him as a heavenly Father. If my life is to bear fruit for His glory I must be able to accept Job's philosophy: "He knows the way I take." That means He is never asleep, never disinterested.

Before an athlete can successfully compete in a sport, be it running, boxing, baseball, swimming, tennis, or whatever, he must undergo a long period of strenuous training. A boxer, for example, must have a sparring partner who will not only help him sharpen his defenses, but will also condition him to take and survive sharp blows to various parts of his body. Without this type of training a boxer would go down under his opponent's first blow.

Yet how many Christians want God to make them great Christians without any training, or hardships, or blows, or adversities! Why, that's like training for a 100-yard dash by sitting in an easy chair and stuffing oneself with rich foods while being waited on hand and foot! How far or how fast do you suppose a person could run after a few months or years of that kind of training?

Effective training for anything worthwhile always involves hardship as an essential ingredient. We Christians live in a world fraught with woe because of Edenic sin; therefore, if we are to be able to succor those with problems and to be "salt" in a decaying world, we must undergo many unpleasant experiences. We are not exempt because we are Christians but we should bear our burdens with greater aplomb because of who we are and because of Who we have!

It is ridiculous to say or think that God is cruel because He allows adversities to come to us. Is a football coach who drives his men to the limits of their strength, who scolds them for their errors, cajoles them into doing their best, and "threatens" them when they goof off, their enemy? Would it be better that he train them by feeding them ice cream sundaes and by fitting up their locker rooms like luxury apartments? If he did that he would be no coach at all. He would, instead, be a fraud and a fool. He would be training his team to fail, not win.

Have you ever seen metal cast in a foundry? A customer places an order for a certain type of metal product. Blueprints are provided which give all the specifications, after which the chief pattern maker makes a wood replica about which the molding sand is shaped. Then the iron ingots are placed in the furnace and melted. The liquid iron is then carried in ladles to the mold and poured. When the iron cools, the mold is set aside.

But the object is far from ready. The rough nodules are chiseled off, after which the entire casing is smoothed and polished on a wheel. It is then placed on a lathe and trimmed to a few hundredths of an inch of what the designer asked for.

It is a long, tough way from the dull gray ingot to the finished product—a lot of heat, pounding, polishing, and finishing. Until it reaches its finished state, it hasn't the faintest idea what it is to be! Only the pattern maker, molder, and machinist know.

God is all three: maker, molder, and machinist. He has a design for us into which we cannot fit without a long, grueling process. But when He is finished with us, we will fit exactly where we should! He doesn't tell us what our final task or purpose is; for that we must trust Him! As Job so aptly put it, "He knows every detail of what is happening to me; and when He has tried me, I shall come forth as pure gold!"

We must not sacrifice
the living for the dead!

11 HOW TO MEET BEREAVEMENT

The famous English clergyman, John Wesley, was once asked the secret of the success of his movement. "Our people," he replied, "die well."

Whether or not a person dies "well," he will die. I realize this is a grim thought, yet there is no sidestepping it. Invariably the day comes when one is taken and the other left. In every city, every day, the grim reaper pays his unwelcomed visit and leaves in his wake a gnawing loneliness that no philosophy of "sweetness and light" can assuage.

During the many years of my experience as a minister I have frequently come across this inevitable event and have observed the divergent reactions of the bereaved. Some are embittered, while others are stunned, unable to grasp the reality of what has taken place. Still others resort to stoicism, appearing, at least outwardly, to be unaffected by their loss. Yet it is inevitable that inner emotions run high at a funeral. Storms of anguish and apprehension rage and a sense of irretrievable loss descends. To lose a dear one is to undergo the deepest emotional experience in all of life.

In what way should we meet this inevitable encounter? Should we resign ourselves to it with a "this-is-the-will-of-God-and-there-is-nothing-I-can-do-about-it" attitude? Or should we give vent to our feelings and mourn uncontrollably, giving full vent to our sense of loss and feeling of frustration?

Obviously no one can predetermine what he or she will say, or how they will respond, when that inevitable hour arrives. Actually, most of us refuse to even anticipate it; we shrug it off as something we will deal with as best we can when the moment arrives.

To suggest that we meet it with gaiety would be to border on the macabre. When Frankie Millier, a 26-year-old gypsy prince, died in Cleveland a few years ago, a five-piece jazz band played "When the Saints Go Marching In," and when the hearse entered the cemetery the band played such songs as "Hello, Dolly," and "Days of Wine and Roses." Friends threw flowers, dirt, beer, wine, whiskey, and money into the open grave. "This is to kill lingering evil spirits," they explained, "and to buy the prince's way into heaven."

What a contrast this is to the unavailing plea of the dead rich man in Luke 16 who cried, "Have mercy on me . . . I am tormented in this flame" (v. 24). It is also in contrast to the words of the psalmist, "And now, Lord, what wait I for? my hope is in thee!" (39:7).

There is a way in which God does not want us to view death, and that is to deny its reality. There are those who refuse to accept it, who cling to their memories, withdraw from society, and live out their years as recluses. While we sympathize with such, we must in all candor say that it is foolish, needless, and a sure formula for the destruction of any further usefulness on the part of the survivor.

Please understand that I am not minimizing the grief associated with the departure of a loved one or a close friend from this life. I have shed my quota of tears over such losses, realizing they are irreplaceable. To this day, with only slight provocation, I can become deeply emotional over the loss of those who in the past have shaped my life and have meant more to me than I could possibly express verbally. But I know, too, that life goes on and that my ministry to others must not stop or be deterred by my sentiments. To become obsessed with the past is to hurt myself and my mission more than it hurts anyone or anything else. So, while I retain all the tender memories, and joyfully anticipate a future reunion, I must not sacrifice the living for the dead!

In His infinite wisdom, God has allowed death to become an integral part of the order of our universe. The sentence upon man is not discriminatory; everything is dying—stars, planets, galaxies—everything. When Adam sinned, death not only passed upon all men, but upon everything. That process will be halted only when Christ returns and establishes a new heaven and a new earth, as He promises in Revelation 21:1.

So many who write me take the attitude that the death of a loved one is punitive. "How could God do this to me?" they ask. Well, let me tell you something, friend: God never takes one life to punish another. I'm not ruling out the possibility that death is sometimes used to melt a stony heart, but remember, God never punishes the innocent to penalize the guilty. I take that back; there was one exception. He sent His innocent Son to Calvary to die for a guilty world. But God would never plunge a soul into hell to save the soul of another. So get it out of your head that the death of a loved one is divine retribution on the living. What God's reasons are for taking a life I cannot say, but it's a matter between God and the deceased. And whatever the reason, total justice is served.

I have found that the best course is to accept death, anyone's death, as the will of God. Don't try to analyze this event. I know the wicked often die old and the godly die young. Bertrand Russell spent the greater part of his ninety-eight years attacking the gospel and assailing Judeo-Christian moral standards. During most of that time he enjoyed good health, and died, I understand, as devoted as ever to his atheistic philosophy.

Conversely, Philip Paul Bliss was a devoted Christian song leader and hymn composer. In December of 1876, when he was only thirty-eight years old, he and his wife boarded a train in Buffalo, New York, bound for Chicago where he was scheduled to participate in a series of gospel meetings. At 8 o'clock that night, as the train approached Ashtabula, Ohio, a railroad bridge collapsed and seven of the cars plunged into an icy river below. Many who would otherwise have escaped drowning were cremated in the fire that broke seconds later. Of the 165 passengers on the ill-fated cars, only 59 bodies were recovered, and only 14 people survived. One survivor reported that Philip Bliss could have escaped, but because his wife was hopelessly caught in the wreckage, he remained at her side and together they succumbed to the onrushing flames. For three days Bliss's friends searched the scene of the disaster looking for his and his wife's remains, but nothing was ever found that could be identified with them.

A hater of the gospel living to ninety-eight; a lover of the gospel dying violently at thirty-eight! How do you account for it? Bertrand Russell, the atheist, has a grave and an epitaph; Bliss has neither. But I can tell you one thing; Bertrand Russell never left the world anything like this:

When peace like a river attendeth my way,
    When sorrows like sea billows roll;
Whatever my lot, Thou hast taught me to say,
    "It is well, it is well, with my soul!"

H. G. Spafford, a Chicago businessman, wrote those words after he received word that four of his five children had drowned in an accident at sea. P. P. Bliss wrote the music.

Admittedly death creates a vacuum, one that it seems, at least for a while, nothing can fill. But God can fill it! Just lean on His promises! For untold millenia they have sustained His people when loved ones have slipped away, never to return to this earthly scene.

Regretfully, this defense mechanism is too seldom put to use by Christians, at least this is the impression I gain as I talk to people and read their letters. Rather than lean on God and His promises, they turn to medicine and psychology. On whom are you leaning, my bereaved friend, God or the pharmacist? Could you survive without the prescription counter? Millions of Christians who preceded you did! They had no sleeping pills or tranquilizers to tide them over these periods of sorrow, but they had something far better: total reliance on a sovereign, loving, understanding God! You can't beat that for therapeutical value!

On a South Vietnam highway a refugee peasant and his wife were trudging southward to escape death at the hands of the Communists. Several of their loved ones had already been massacred. Ta Hop Toan was the husband, and he was a Christian. An American reporter asked him what Christmas meant to him (it was the Christmas season). His reply was, "It means that Christ came to earth to help the poor." "And has He helped you?" was the next question. "Yes," replied the weary peasant, "He gave me strength to carry my children." He had carried them thirty miles! His wife, also a Christian and wounded, had brought two more children and a few belongings. "He gave me strength," she added, "to walk in pain."

The dedicated Christian finds strength to walk, not without pain, but in pain and without despair! Dare any of us complain when we compare our lot with that of Ta Hop Toan and his family? They had lost nearly all their relatives and possessions, yet they were able to say of Jesus, "He came to help the poor and to give us strength."

A poet whose name I do not know wrote the following:

> I would to God I knew some place
>   Where I could lock my love away
> Secure from death, whose quiet face
>   Looked in upon us yesterday.
> But lovers have nowhere to hide:
>   We cannot creep beneath a leaf
> Or find a crack and slip inside
>   Beyond the fingers of this thief.
>
> No bolted door, no cunning mesh
>   Of woven steel, no wall of stone
> Can shield the petal of the flesh
>   Or save the living stem of bone.
> But only this—if we possess
>   A love as strong and sure as death!
>
> What matters one heartbeat the less?
>   One pitiable pinch of breath?
> Death cannot grasp the sun, nor cup
>   His bony hand around the sea,
> Nor take love to lift it up
>   From earth to eternity.

A beautiful sentiment we all agree. But it is no substitute for the Christian hope, a hope far beyond rhetoric, a hope safe within the fold of the Christian's loving Father!

Knowing the rules is one thing:
obeying them is quite another.

12 STAYING "ON THE BEAM"

"On the beam" is an expression that had its genesis in the modern science of aeronautics. When a pilot is on course he is said to be "on the beam." If he strays off the beam, he must quickly analyze his problem and adjust his course, for correction time is rigidly limited in the air. It isn't like someone in an automobile taking the wrong road.

The world teems with people who are "off the beam" morally and spiritually, yet there is an amazingly limited amount of concern expressed, either privately or publicly, about this perilous condition. Obviously many feel there is ample time in which to make the necessary corrections. In fact, I fear we are dying of "plenty-of-timitis!" Like a pilot whose instruments malfunction and who loses contact with the ground, we have lost our corporate contact with spiritual reality. And again I say, the greatest danger lies in the fact that we think there is "plenty of time" in which to get back on course.

Living, however, is not as simple as flying. Today there are sophisticated instruments that all but fly an airplane without human help, instruments that can take a plane off and bring it down without a human hand at the controls. But when it comes to controling men, we are no closer to success socially and politically than the Greeks were in Homer's day!

The pilot who stays on the beam can either watch a gyrocompass, or listen for a steady beeping sound in his headset. But what do we look at, and listen for, when we attempt to stay on the beam morally and spiritually?

First we must be able to recognize the signs which indicate that we are off course. In the case of the pilot with his headphones, the sign is silence. But in the case of a life, the signs are many and varied. It is necessary to analyze many things carefully. For example, what do we laugh at? What makes us cry? Around what do our thoughts center? How do we spend our time?

If you laugh heartily and spontaneously at a dirty joke, you are off the beam and need a new sense of direction. Do you treat lightly the misfortunes of others, people who are humiliated, sensitive people who have been hurt deeply? If so, you are having navigational troubles. Do you pout or complain bitterly over minor defeats and insults? If so, your instruments are malfunctioning. You are obviously unduly occupied with yourself. In simpler terms, you are "off the beam!"

As a pilot, I know the importance of maps and navigational instruments. I know, too, that above all else one must have contact with the ground. Many a pilot, with instruments awry, has been "talked down," but to lose radio contact with mother earth is probably the most serious situation in which a pilot can find himself. I know there was a time when pilots flew, as we say, by "the seat of their pants," but many of them never lived to write a book about it! Moreover, the air was not then filled with planes and there were fewer "concrete jungles." Then every hayfield and cornfield was a landing strip. Today they are not.

To get a pilot's license one must do one thing above

all others, he must learn the rules! There are certain procedures which the Federal Aviation Agency insists on. Failure to comply can result in grounding, temporarily or permanently. Try to imagine the resultant confusion if, after learning to pilot a plane, the pilot were told he was "on his own," that his chief concern thereafter was to save his own skin! Let me tell you, flying is difficult enough with all the rules. Imagine aviation without regulations! No one in his right mind would suggest that each pilot be a law unto himself. Yet this is the essence of what many highly regarded educators are saying with respect to the moral world!

If a pilot must abide by rules to save his own life and the lives of others, what about the rules for living? Would anyone with a grain of intelligence suggest that everyone be turned loose to do "his own thing," to be ethical only as a given situation demands? When you hear a theologian advocate "situation ethics," remember he is suggesting that we abandon the Rule Book and "interpret" individual situations in the light of their respective moral value. In other words, they are telling a pilot to ignore the manual and control tower!

Only one guidebook in the history of the world has met all the demands of ethics, conscience, morality, and human obligation. That book is the Bible. For thousands of years men have tried to surpass it, even match it, but without success. The Bible is to the soul what a book on anatomy is to a doctor, what a book on chemistry is to a pharmacist, what a book on mathematics is to a banker, and what a grammar book is to a journalist!

The first rule for staying "on the beam" is self-renunciation. Jesus said, "If any man would come after me, let him deny himself and take up his cross and follow me" (Matt. 16:24). He also said, "The man who loves his own life will destroy it, and the man who hates his life in this world will preserve it for eternal life" (John 12:25, *Phillips*). So the first step is the crucifixion of ego, the renunciation of all the so-called "rights" of one's little self. Which of His "rights" did Jesus protect? His concern was for others.

What a different world ours would be if everyone had an eager concern for the rights of others! There is so much self-assertion but so little self-renunciation. Many who are bent on having their own way are prepared to start a riot, burn a city, kill a policeman, torment, heckle, and harrass any with whom they disagree. The question as far as they are concerned is not, "Is this right or wrong?" but, "Is this what I want?" This is the lowest possible form of self-love.

Someone has suggested that the reason some people become so depressed when they are sick is that they think they are too important to be sick!

Are you bored with any voice but your own? If so, it may be because you think yours is the only one worth listening to. My, what navigational troubles a mis-directed ego can touch off! Most problems stem from a perverted sense of self-importance. Only when self is where it belongs—on the altar—can it be said we are "on the beam." The self some people guard so zealously may some day be the means of their everlasting undoing!

It is not enough, however, to renounce self; we must replace it if we are to stay "on the beam." When a public official leaves office, or is defeated at the polls, that office is not left vacant. Someone fills it. It is not enough to lop off bad habits or evil thoughts; they must be replaced with good habits and good thoughts. In other words, a new tenant must occupy the vacancy left by the eviction.

This is what Jesus meant when He told in Luke 24 about the unclean spirit who left a man, then was replaced by seven others "more wicked than himself" (v. 45). He was referring to those who believe that "getting religion" is simply ditching bad habits and evil companions, then turning over a new leaf. But we need

78

to do more than resist evil; we must embrace good! Many dissipate their energies by merely keeping the door closed against the man in the basement. That's negative. The Christian is to accentuate the positive. He not only sweeps away the rubbish and wipes off the dust, but he moves someone else in quickly, for he knows that some spirit will inhabit him, and it will be either from heaven or from hell!

I would like to be able to suggest a neat little package of rules that would guarantee the enthronement of Christ and the dethronement of self, but it isn't quite that simple. The process involves more than a mere increase in knowledge, more than merely going to church oftener, or praying more fervently, or reading a chapter in the Bible every day. The renunciation of self is rather like going on a diet. Most of us overweight people know the rules. We've studied the calorie charts; we know all about high protein, low fat, and no carbohydrates. Yes, we know the calorie charts right down to their last little number! But knowing the facts doesn't take off the weight.

Knowing the rules for staying on the beam spiritually is one thing. Obeying them is another. I can tell you, and I can tell myself, what is essential to becoming a spiritual Christian, but many who know all the answers make the biggest mess of their lives. Of course we must first know, but knowledge is worthless unless we do.

When I was learning to fly, two very important rules were drilled into me. The first was that I was to trust my instruments, particularly my compass, above my own hunches. The other was that I must keep checking with the ground for weather conditions, wind direction and velocity, and for information about other planes in the vicinity. No pilot has enough natural "instincts" to stay out of trouble forever. As a Christian, I find that I cannot operate my life successfully without help, not from the ground, but from the sky! There is a fisherman's prayer that goes like this: "Lord, have mercy on me; my boat is so little, and Thy ocean is so great."

Life, too, is vast, and we are microscopic by comparison. We can never stay "on the beam" without divine help. And that is undoubtedly why Paul said, "For to me to live is Christ." With Him as our copilot, we'll never get off the beam!

Most cases
of misplaced faith and mistaken judgment
are reversible.

13 PRIME THE PUMP

There was this old baking powder can, tied to an old water pump on a seldom-used back trail in the Amargosa Desert, better known as Death Valley. The letter, yellowed by the elements, read:

This pump is all right as of June, 1932. I put a new sucker washer on it and it ought to last five years. But the washer dries out and the pump has got to be primed. Under the white rock I buried a bottle of water, out of the sun and cork up. There's enough water in it to prime the pump, but not if you drink some first.

Pour about one-fourth and let her soak and wet the leather. Then pour in the rest medium fast and pump like crazy. You'll git water. The well has never run dry. Have faith. When you git watered up, fill the bottle and put it back like you found it for the next feller.

(signed) Desert Pete

P.S. Don't go drinking up the water first. Prime the pump with it and you'll get all you can hold.

This true story has all the makings of a first class lesson on faith. Get the picture: a prospector is trudging along a desert trail, exhausted, canteen empty. Suddenly he comes across this old pump and reads Desert Pete's letter. What he does thereafter will tell us what kind of a man he is, a man of faith or a man of suspicion. In this case, faith will have to be a good deal more than a theological definition or discussion; it will be something upon which his very life depends.

Plausible faith requires at least two components, the first of which is a dependable object. One hears a lot of trivia these days about the need to believe in oneself, and to have faith in one's fellowman. But when has faith in oneself ever turned a bad nature around? Or when has faith in one's fellowman ever kept a stick-up man from pulling the trigger? The little jingle, "Just have faith," is supposed to cheer everyone up and save the world from itself; but can't you see how meaningless it is unless its object is a reliable thing or person? Faith always helps, but only when it's bilateral. It is by no means a magical panacea for the world's ills, something that will keep children out of trouble and adults away from each other's throats.

Of course we all want people to believe in us, but my faith in a person will not change his heart. Many a parent has had his or her heart broken by children they trusted. Britain and Russia trusted Nazi Germany, but that didn't prevent World War II. Some people don't seem to understand that our faith in the leaders in Hanoi will never cause them to change their marxist philosophies or abandon their aggressive designs in Indo-China. If you think I am wrong, stick around a while and see.

In the case of Desert Pete's letter in the old baking powder can, the stranger who benefits from its instructions must trust a man entirely unknown to him. What guarantee has the man, perishing with thirst, that Desert Pete even exists, to say nothing of the reliability of his instructions concerning the priming of the pump? What proof, in fact, does he have that there is even water in the well?

Would it be worth the chance? What would you do? It would be interesting to know just how many people, through the years, believed that yellowed note and entrusted their lives to it.

What would I do if I were dying of thirst and came across the pump, Pete's letter, and the bottle of water under the rock? I don't know. Who really knows until he finds himself in those circumstances? Certainly a lot of factors would have to be weighed, but from where I now sit, with food and drink no problem, I believe I would trust Desert Pete's instructions. I would have to believe that no man, especially a grizzled old desert prospector who must have known the pangs of hunger and thirst, would trick a man to his death on those burning sands!

So I would hazard the guess that most people would agree that one would have a better chance to survive by trusting Desert Pete's instructions. But it is also clear to everyone that the note could have been a hoax, or the pump "sucker," as Pete called it, had deteriorated sooner than he figured, or the well had meanwhile gone dry. In other words the object of faith here was a fallible man, and fallibility spells the possibility of human error.

Next, faith always involves the element of risk. Everyone agrees it would be a risk to use precious water to prime a pump whose idiosyncrasies one had no way of determining beforehand. I know from experience that faith in man sometimes has its pitfalls. A few people I have trusted have fooled, gypped, and disappointed me. Fortunately, my lack of discernment thus far has not been fatal; I may be bloody, but I'm unbowed! Most cases of misplaced faith and mistaken judgment are reversible. But in any event, life teems with risks, "risks of faith," if you wish to call them that.

We take a risk every time we climb into an automobile, or eat in a restaurant, or walk into a darkened room, or any number of ordinary things. Yes, life is filled with calculated risks.

The Caribbean island republic of Haiti is one of the most poverty-stricken nations in the world. It is plagued with droughts, hurricanes, and depleted soil. Thousands of Haitians have died from malnutrition and outright starvation. Yet in the midst of these food crises the wiser Haitians save some of their corn for seed. I have often seen ears of corn hanging high in trees, hopefully safe from marauding neighbors and rats. That corn might save a few lives temporarily, but if kept till planting time it produces enough new corn to save many lives for many months.

How can a husband and father keep that seed corn out of reach when his family is hungry? It's a chance he must take. He might lose; but his chances of gaining (and thus living) are 50-50, and he can't afford not to take the risk.

When I ask you to trust Jesus Christ as your Savior, it involves a risk, to be sure, for to this point you can't be sure (even though I can!). But the nice thing about this risk is you can't lose. If you are right you have lost nothing, but have gained everything. But if you don't take the risk, the step of faith—and you are wrong in your refusal or neglect—you will lose everything!

Moreover, it is only after the initial step of faith is taken that anyone can know whether he is right or wrong. The only convinced people are those who have believed. Remember the postscript on Pete's note? "Don't go drinking up the water first. Prime the pump with it and you'll get all you can hold." The thirsty traveler had to give up something before he could get something. Before you can partake of the Water of Life freely, you must give up something: your pride, your will, your doubts, your love of sin. But what you get in return will astound and delight you! Jesus said, "There is no man that has left house, or parents, or brethren, or wife, or children, for the kingdom of God's sake, who will not receive much more in this present time, and in the world to come life everlasting" (Luke 18:29,30). That's a double-barreled guarantee if I ever saw one! But first you must trust Jesus Christ, just as the desert traveler would trust Desert Pete for that abundant supply of water. Christ has taken all the risk out of trusting Him by rising from the dead. "Because I live, you shall live also," He told His disciples (John 14:19).

You say, "But I don't take risks." Come on, now; who do you think you're kidding? Everyone takes risks: people who bank their money, people who ride in cars, trains, and planes, farmers who plant crops, people who venture into business for themselves; in fact, anyone you can think of takes risks. Many risks involve only money or health; this risk involves the soul. You must make a decision either for or against Christ. It's better to lose a crop than to lose out on heaven. It's better to lose your life than to miss out on Christ, for when Christians lose their lives they merely exchange faith for sight! And that, says Paul, is "far better."

We take more risks after we become Christians than we do initially. Why, I almost get palpitation of the heart when I look back on some of the projects I've undertaken since becoming a Christian! But the faith that saved me has carried me through. God doesn't label His miracles Hard, Harder, and Hardest!

Understand, now, that faith doesn't preclude hard work. Eternal life is free, but accomplishments thereafter call for unrelentingly hard work. I have never known a successful preacher who was lazy, or vice versa (a principle that applies in every line of endeavor). First the plunge of faith, then work—hard, hard work!

Nicholas Murray Butler once said, "I divide the world into three classes: the few who make things happen, the many who watch things happen, and the overwhelming majority who have no notion of what happens." If we properly exercise faith, we will belong to the minority group that "makes things happen." "Without faith, it is impossible to please God" (Heb.11:6).

> A traveler crossed a frozen stream
> In a trembling fear one day.
> Later a teamster drove across
> And whistled all the way.
>
> Great faith and little faith alike
> Were granted safe convoy,
> But one had pangs of needless fear,
> The other all the joy.

Believe me,
we all come under the crushing weight of disappointment
sooner or later.

14 HOW TO HANDLE DISAPPOINTMENT

Someone has said, "No man, with a man's heart in him, gets far on his way without some bitter, soul-searching disappointment." It goes without saying that this does not apply to men only. It applies to both men and women, and to young people as well.

I would not want assigned to me the task of controlling divine providence or ordering the events of my own life, but I would be less than honest if I did not confess that there have been times when I felt I could improve on what God has permitted to come to pass. Let's face it; much of the history of mankind has been written in the language of cruel disappointment. On the plus side, however, there are those heroic souls who have not allowed adversity to crush them and who have, through their own determination and the grace of God, triumphed in its face.

Some of the most colorful examples of disappointment come to us from the pages of the Bible and history. As all know who have studied Israel's early history, her great leader, Moses, had an all-consuming desire to lead his people to the land of promise. They

87

went in, but Moses died outside its borders. It was David's ardent hope that he would be permitted to build the great temple for God's glory, and for years he gathered treasure and drew plans. But David died before one stone of its foundation was laid. Most of the patriarchs, including Abraham and Jeremiah, were denied their loftiest aspirations. Paul had a coveted preaching mission cancelled by divine decree.

Abraham Lincoln longed for the day when he could see his nation reunited in peace and prosperity, but an assassin's bullet cut him down before he experienced that satisfaction. Samuel Mills, who founded the American Board of Commissioners for Foreign Missions, had a burning desire to reach the continent of Africa for Christ. But he died at age thirty-five on his return trip from Africa where he had gone to select a site for a missionary colony.

All of these I have mentioned, plus countless others, would have changed things had they been able to manage their own affairs. And there is little doubt but that each wondered, when the dream faded, why it had to be so.

Many of you have suffered thwarted ambitions; you have had blighted dreams; you have tried to reach the top rung of the ladder of your profession, only to see others pass and surpass you in the race while you remained a relatively mediocre and disappointed person. Or maybe your material possessions have been swept away through bad investments, or crushing medical costs, or disasterous inflation. After seeing your carefully laid and treasured plans crumble, you are now aware of the hopelessness of thinking in terms of real security for the future. Or maybe your health is broken and nothing known to medical science holds out hope for you. So today you are asking, "Does God care? If so, would He let this happen to me?"

Believe me, we all come under the crushing weight of

88

disappointment sooner or later. Sometimes it comes as a thief in the night, robbing us, and appearing to leave us very poor indeed. Sometimes we can think of our lives only in terms of shipwreck, with shattered ambitions and unrealized dreams scattered everywhere. And always there is that little rise of resentment and the question, "Why?"

While I have learned a bit less in my lifetime than I should have, one thing I have learned is that it does no good to try to analyze why certain things happen. I am now aware, as never before, that I not only cannot understand everything; I need not understand! If I am to accept the sovereignty of God, which I do, I must leave the "why" to Him. But I can do more than that. I can ask Him to strengthen me, to make me a better man because of disappointment. To put it tritely, I have learned to accept disappointment as "His appointment."

One of the best examples of how not to handle disappointment is handed down to us in the Bible in an event that took place some 900 years before Christ. It has to do with a very famous Israeli prophet by the name of Elijah. First Kings 19:4 contains a quote with which every student of the Bible is familiar: "It is enough; now, O Lord, take away my life."

If those sound like the words of a very disappointed man, it is because they are. Elijah was so disappointed and frightened he wanted to die. (Sound familiar?) But God had planned it so Elijah wouldn't die at all but would be taken to heaven in a blazing chariot with wheels of flame and horses of fire. What an honor for Elijah! How happy he must have been that his childish, cowardly prayer was not answered.

Elijah had concluded that his life was a failure. This is actually quite strange, for only the day before he had had a successful encounter with the priests of Baal, and the people, with one voice, had acknowledged Jehovah as the only true God. It then looked like a permanent victory for Israel's God, but now the cup of success that had touched Elijah's lips lay shattered at his feet. The prophet was so discouraged he wanted to die!

You see, Queen Jezebel was not at all happy about the demise of the prophets of Baal, so she sent this message to Elijah: "You killed my prophets, and now I swear by the gods that I am going to kill you by this time tomorrow night" (I Kings 19:2, *The Living Bible*).

So Elijah fled for his life. We regret this dark chapter in the life of this great and godly man. I wish he had stood up to the imperious queen and dared her to do her worst, but the Bible is a book written about human beings as they were, not as they should have been. It records their weaknesses as well as their conquests, and obviously Elijah was caught here at the wrong time.

Nevertheless, if it is true that discretion is the better part of valor, Elijah may not have been as much in error as we at first think. After all, even Jesus eluded His enemies at times, as did the apostle Paul. What was wrong was Elijah's lament, "It is enough; now, O Lord, let me die." God didn't say, "It is enough;" Elijah did. Elijah may have been through with life, but God wasn't through with Elijah! The underlying reason for the discrepancy between the two views is that God knew the future and Elijah didn't.

Isn't that usually the difference between us and God? As I look back over my life I recall a number of instances when I felt just as Elijah did, although I may have expressed it differently. Yet in the light of subsequent events, I am glad God didn't come running to do my bidding. We all have occasional depressions, but they are only temporary. What appears catastrophic today may seem like an opportunity tomorrow!

One of the worst blunders we can make is to make major decisions in times of depression and disappointment. There is always a certain amount of irrationality which accompanies depression. Under the weight of bitter disappointment no one thinks clearly. But sanity will return, so let's learn to play the waiting game. Disappointments and seeming failures are often doorways through which we enter into a larger and fuller life.

I have referred briefly to Paul's disappointment. He wanted to go eastward to Spain. He had, in fact, made elaborate plans for that missionary journey. But God blocked the way and sent him westward instead, where his ministry favorably affected the whole program of the gospel for centuries to come.

David Livingstone originally planned to go to China, but God sent him to Africa. His disappointment gave him a tomb and a tablet in Westminster Abbey and immortalized his name.

Ulysses Grant failed as a farmer, as a real estate salesman, and couldn't even get an appointment as a county engineer. By his own admission he wasn't even a successful clerk in his father's store! But he rose to fame as the greatest general of his day.

Lincoln knew disappointment as few men have known it. He failed in commercial life, being unable to run even a small grocery store successfully. He failed in military life, going into the Black Hawk War a captain and coming out a private! He failed several times to get elected to political office. But these were stepping-stones however rough, and Lincoln is now immortalized as one of our nation's greatest presidents.

I hear people grumbling about life's adversities, blaming them on everyone from God down to their alderman; but I tell you a life without adversity and disappointment is a life without character. The English oak is coveted by shipbuilders the world over because of what storms and strong winds have put into it. So with the storms of life. As we constantly wrestle against the winds of opposition, we are adding muscle to our character.

Have you suffered a bitter disappointment? If so,

how are you reacting? Are you saying as Elijah did, "I've had enough, Lord. Take away my life. I must die sometime, and it may as well be now." Oh, let me assure you there's a better course than that! Kneel before the great Burden-bearer, He who suffered disappointment and heartache and cruelty and privation for the whole human race, and find in the light of His sufferings and disappointments the best interpretation of your own. Only then will you be able to say with the great apostle Paul: I have learned, in whatsoever state I am, therewith to be content!" (Phil. 4:11).